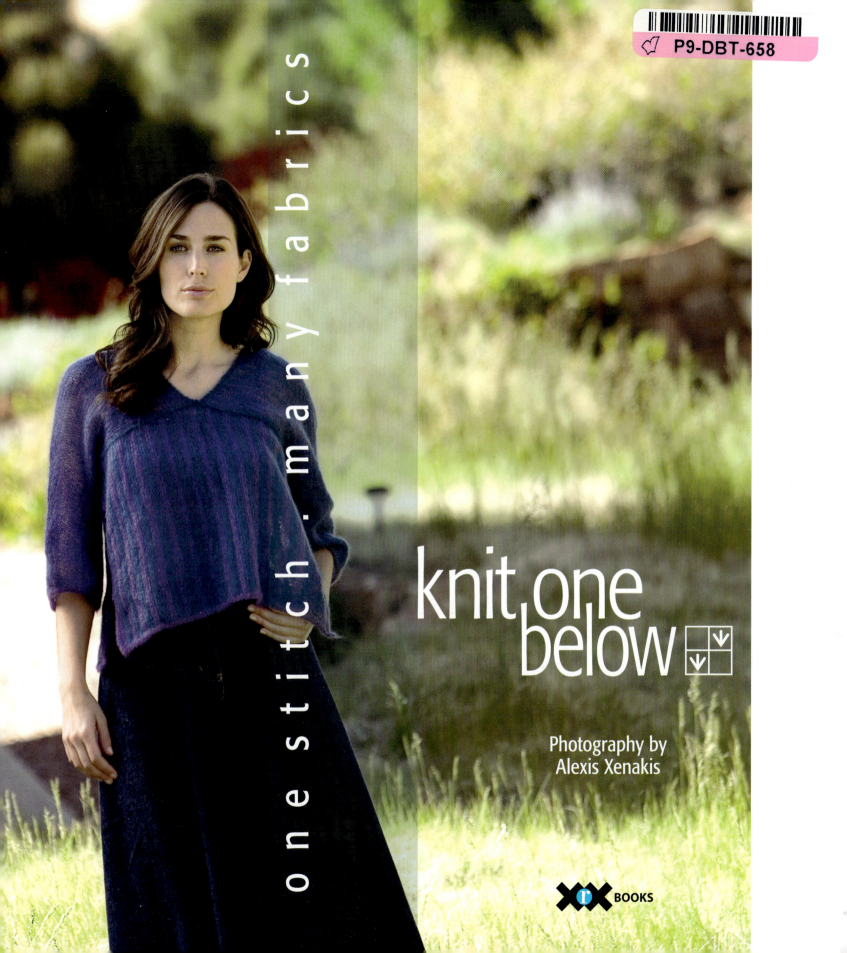

one stitch . many fabrics

knit one
below

Photography by
Alexis Xenakis

XRX BOOKS

PUBLISHER
Alexis Yiorgos Xenakis

EDITOR
Elaine Rowley

FASHION AND KNITTING EDITOR
Rick Mondragon

MANAGING EDITOR
Karen Bright

TECHNICAL EDITORS
Sue Nelson
Beth Whiteside

EDITORIAL COORDINATOR
Elisabeth Robinson

GRAPHIC DESIGNER
Bob Natz

PHOTOGRAPHER
Alexis Yiorgos Xenakis

PHOTO STYLIST
Lisa Mannes

CHIEF EXECUTIVE OFFICER
Benjamin Levisay

DIRECTOR, PUBLISHING SERVICES
David Xenakis

TECHNICAL ILLUSTRATOR
Carol Skallerud

PRODUCTION DIRECTOR & COLOR SPECIALIST
Dennis Pearson

BOOK PRODUCTION MANAGER
Greg Hoogeveen

DIGITAL PREPRESS
Everett Baker

MARKETING MANAGER
Lisa Mannes

BOOKS DISTRIBUTION
Mavis Smith

MIS
Jason Bittner

SECOND PRINTING, 2009; FIRST PUBLISHED IN USA IN 2008 BY XRX, INC.

We give permission to readers to photocopy the instructions and graphics for personal use only.
ISBN 13: 978–193306413-0
ISBN 10: 193306413-7
Produced in Sioux Falls, South Dakota, by XRX, Inc.,
PO Box 965, Sioux Falls, SD 57101-965 USA
605.338.2450

a publication of  BOOKS
visit us online — knittinguniverse.com

DEDICATION

This book is dedicated to two elderly Dutch ladies who deserve special mention. The first one is my mother, Taetske Duvekot who, in the best tradition of passing down knowledge and skills from one generation to the next, taught me how to knit when I was a child and inspired in me a fondness for the magical and extremely rewarding activity that knitting is. Who knows, if it weren't for her I might never have taken up knitting in the first place and that would indeed have been a great loss for me.

The other person is my friend Nelly van Panhuis, whose sharp mind and great enthusiasm for knitting accompanied me at every step along the way, as she discovered her own creativity and encouraged mine while knitting projects for this book.

Vests 2

Jackets 20

Sweaters 38

Wardrobe Building 58

a publication of XRX **BOOKS**

knit one below

Elise Duvekot

Creature Comforts 76

Child & Baby 90

Head to Toe 104

Features & Highlights

From its humble beginnings as a purely utilitarian craft, knitting has evolved into a true art form, encompassing elements of design, fashion, and craftsmanship. With an eye toward upholding this time-honored tradition, I have built upon what has come before and written this book for all knitters, from the novice to the expert. New knitters will discover a stitch pattern that is straightforward to learn as they expand their skills in projects that are exciting to make, while more experienced knitters will be amazed at the effects they can achieve by incorporating this new technique into their work. I hope that this book will lend wings to knitters' imaginations.

Knitting into the stitch below (k1b) has been overlooked as a design element, appearing only sporadically in projects and in a few stitch dictionaries. In fact, many knitting glossaries neither mention the k1b stitch, nor do they assign a symbol or abbreviation to it. In writing this book, I have endeavored to shine a spotlight on this almost forgotten stitch. I set out on what became a quest, a journey of true discovery. Along the way, I devised new ways to use the k1b stitch, striving to elevate it to its rightful place in the knitting universe, and turn it into an invaluable instrument in the knitter's design toolbox.

As the title *Knit One Below: One Stitch, Many Fabrics* suggests, every project in this book uses the technique of knitting into the stitch below. This 'One Stitch' is k1b—knit one into the stitch below—when worked on one side of the fabric and p1b—purl one into the stitch below—when worked on the opposite side, the two forming an identical stitch. The 'Many Fabrics' are the multifaceted results: when the k1b stitch pattern is worked in a single yarn, it produces a more subdued fabric, while the two-yarn approach, the Column Pattern, brings the color versatility of this stitch to the fore.

This novel stitch will appeal to knitters who love color work and to those who enjoy learning new techniques. The projects range from the simple to the more complex as you build on the basic stitch. Once you can knit one below and purl one below, you can make any of the projects in this book—and venture beyond.

The K1b Journey

I have often been asked how I came up with this idea. Did I just think it up one fine day? It wasn't quite like that. A while back, I was working on some socks with two contrasting colors of yarn, experimenting with slipping and stranding to mingle the two colors, but the fabric was turning out tight and stiff. I tried knitting into the stitch below and noticed that the stitch had become a bit wider and looser; at the same time, the color from the previous row had been drawn upwards and the color on my needle had fallen out of sight to the back of the fabric. As I alternated the k1b stitch with a regular knit stitch, the colors started to build vertical columns, and before I knew it, I had made my first pair of k1b socks! More soon followed. Then I set out to work back and forth to make a flat fabric. The eureka moment came with the use of the p1b stitch on the wrong side of the piece. The Column Pattern had been born, and the genie had been let out of the bottle.

The Column Pattern: statuesque columns on one side, flying swallows on the other! Hard to believe that this is one and the same fabric.

Knitting Below

The two-color Column Pattern is extremely easy to work. Each row makes use of only one color. There is no slipping or stranding. There are no yarn-overs or knitting together. Whether the k1b stitch pattern is worked with just one yarn or with two, the fabric looks somewhat like a rib. But a rib entails alternating knits and purls and moving your working yarn from front to back, while the k1b stitch pattern has the same relaxing rhythm as stockinette stitch. Usually, knit and k1b stitches are worked on the right side, while purl and p1b stitches are worked on the wrong side, so that each row involves only one type of stitch—a knit-based stitch or a purl-based stitch. The only difference between a k1 and a k1b (or a p1 and a p1b) is the place where you insert the needle. For the rest, the sequence of motions and the rhythm are exactly the same as in regular knitting.

Stitches and rows in the k1b stitch pattern are easy to count because of the clear stitch definition. Horizontally, they are wide and well-defined, especially when they have been worked in the two-color Column Pattern. Vertically, each visible stitch is elongated in comparison to a regular knit stitch since it corresponds to two worked rows. As you drop the k1b stitch from your left needle, the stitch that was above it on the needle slides off. In a manner of speaking, that stitch becomes a float that lies out of sight behind the stitch below.

The Fabric

The fabric created by knitting one below has a distinctive hand. It is never tight, stiff, or unyielding. On the contrary, it is supple, drapes well, and can be worked loosely or tightly, thus making it suitable for many different purposes. It qualifies as a jack-of-all-trades since it can be incorporated into a wide variety of techniques—cables, intarsia, knit-purl combinations, mitered squares, beading—and lends itself to a broad range of projects—sweaters, shawls, socks and more—as you will discover.

A welcome feature is that the fabric lies flat and has very little curl. This gives the knitter a great deal of design freedom since edgings and borders are not needed to tame the fabric. It also makes it much easier to handle the individual pieces of a garment when the time comes to assemble it.

Another plus point has to do with appearance: many knitters will relate to the slimming effect of vertical columns as opposed to the horizontal stripes so often seen in knitting projects.

One more welcome surprise: working the k1b stitch is easy on the hands. My theory is that the 'one-two' rhythm interrupts the repetitive motion that can plague knitters when they knit conventional stockinette or garter stitch patterns. Moreover, the k1b stitch is not worked terribly tightly, making it quite relaxing to do. With its 'one-two' rhythm, the Column Pattern is based on pairs—pairs of colors (A and B), pairs of stitches (k1 and k1b as well as p1 and p1b), and pairs of rows (two RS rows, two WS rows).

The Column Pattern

The Column Pattern forms the basis of many of the projects in *Knit One Below*. It is made using two colors in alternating rows. The resulting pattern looks intricate, and people will wonder how you created it. Yet it is much easier to produce than it appears, since only one color at a time is used in each row. After a few rows, it becomes quite obvious which stitch is to be worked next; your knitting will speak to you. When you are working a Color A row, you go below into the Color A columns and when you are working a Color B row, you go below into the Color B columns. Just match up your colors: it is as simple as that.

At first glance, the pattern looks somewhat like stranded knitting, but the crucial difference is that there is no need to work two colors at the same time. Fair Isle patterns that alternate two colors to create striped patterns tend not to have a great deal of elasticity. Slip stitches are sometimes used to create a similar striped effect, but the result also tends to be tight. In contrast, the k1b stitch fabric always stays soft and pliable.

On one side of the fabric, the two colors line up neatly in columns of color or texture. The reverse side is completely different, but with its lovely V-shaped pattern, it is also attractive, making the stitch ideal for afghans, scarves, the lapels of cardigans or jackets, and other projects where both the front and the back of the fabric are visible. With k1b, there is nothing wrong with the wrong side!

The k1b stitch patterns can be worked back and forth or in the round. Working in the round has the advantage that it does not involve purling, you can always see what you are doing, and besides, many knitters prefer to knit rather than purl.

Gauge

The ratio of stitches-to-rows in the k1b stitch pattern depends on the specific yarns used, but it is in the range of about 1-to-3 (1 stitch per 3 rows), very different from the 2-to-3 (or 5-to-7) ratio often found in stockinette stitch. Compared to a stockinette stitch, a k1b stitch is wider and shorter. These differences are very evident in the samples shown, which were all knit with the same yarn.

To give an example, a typical stockinette swatch might have a gauge of 18 stitches × 26 rows = 4", while a k1b swatch made in the same yarn using the same needle size would be more in the vicinity of 12 stitches × 38 rows = 4".

The wider stitch gauge of the k1b pattern means that fewer stitches will be needed to obtain the desired width. You will be surprised to learn that adult socks, for instance, are worked over just 40 stitches rather than the more customary 60.

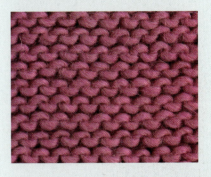

From top to bottom:
With same yarn and needles, 9 stitches and 18 rows worked in stockinette stitch, garter stitch, and Column Pattern.

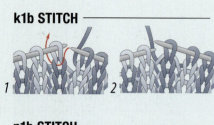

k1b STITCH

1   *2*

p1b STITCH

1   *2*

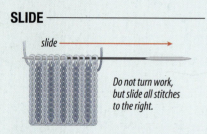

SLIDE

slide →

Do not turn work, but slide all stitches to the right.

NOTE:
Must use circular or double-pointed needles.

The Stitch

The k1b stitch is worked as follows:
1 Instead of knitting into the next stitch on the left needle, knit into the stitch directly below it.
2 Pull the stitch off the left needle and let it drop as you would for a regular knit stitch.

The p1b stitch is worked as follows:
1 Instead of purling into the next stitch on the left needle, purl into the stitch directly below it.
2 Pull the stitch off the left needle and let it drop as you would for a regular purl stitch.

Written instructions and charts

In written or chart form, the instructions are straightforward and easy to follow.

☐ K on RS, p on WS
▾ K1b on RS, p1b on WS
⌄ Slip 1 with yarn on WS

Column Pattern worked over an odd number of stitches (2 yarns)

With color A and using long-tail loop cast-on, cast on an odd number of stitches.
Join B at tail-end of needle and purl across row (A and B are at same end of needle).
Row 1 (RS) With A, k1, *k1, k1b; repeat from *, end k2, slide.
Row 2 (RS) With B, k1, *k1b, k1; repeat from *, turn.
Row 3 (WS) With A, p1, *p1, p1b; repeat from *, end p2, slide.
Row 4 (WS) With B, p1, *p1b, p1; repeat from *, turn.
Outlined squares are the repeat.

Column Pattern

2-st repeat

K1b Pattern worked over an even number of stitches (1 yarn)

Row 1 (RS) Slip 1 as if to purl and with yarn on WS (slip 1), *k1, k1b; repeat from *, end k1.
Row 2 (WS) Slip 1, *p1, p1b; repeat from *, end p1.
Repeat rows 1–2 for K1b Pattern.

K1b Pattern

2-st repeat

Circular Column Pattern worked over an even number of stitches (2 yarns)

With Color A and using long-tail loop cast-on, cast on an even number of stitches.
Join B at tail-end of needle and knit across row (A and B are at same end of needle).
Work the color change loosely, without twisting the yarns around each other.
Round 1 (RS) With A, *k1, k1b; repeat from *
Round 2 (RS) With B, *k1b, k1; repeat from *

Circular Column Pattern

2-st repeat

Circular K1b Pattern worked over an odd number of stitches (1 yarn)

Round 1 (RS) *K1, k1b; repeat from *, end k1.
Round 2 (RS) *K1b, k1; repeat from *, end k1b

Circular K1b Pattern

2-st repeat

Casting on

A loose cast-on is needed for this stitch pattern, since the k1b stitch is wider than regular knits and purls. Commonly used methods such as the long-tail cast-on will make the start too tight, and the stitches above it will not spread out sufficiently.

I launched a search for the optimal cast-on to be used with the k1b stitch pattern. A good candidate appeared to be the loop (e-wrap) cast-on since its ability to stretch laterally allows it to adjust to the width of the stitch. The loop cast-on has often been maligned, and with quite good reason. After all, in stockinette stitch, it yields a loose cast-on that provides very little stability to the lower edge of the knit piece. This cast-on is normally worked towards the ball of yarn, with the yarn becoming twisted or untwisted as you progress. The task at hand was to refine this method in order to overcome its drawbacks.

The k1b stitch pattern is worked on circular or double-pointed needles, and this turned out to be the key to the 'long-tail loop cast-on' method that I have developed for many of the projects. By measuring off a length of yarn and casting on **toward the tail**, you can allow the tail to dangle freely after every few cast-on stitches. The yarn will retain its integrity, it will be restored to exactly its natural and original amount of twist, and the long-tail loop cast-on will be just right: your yarn will not become distressed, distorted, or disjointed.

This sleek cast-on adds very little bulk to your work, disappearing discretely behind your fabric and adding minimal volume, so it lends itself well to picking up stitches as you add edgings later on. A number of the projects start with a loop cast-on using a doubled strand of yarn and, since the k1b fabric lies flat, this cast-on functions perfectly as a finished lower edging.

If you would like a pronounced and well-defined cast-on, you can use the long-tail method by casting on one-and-a-half or two times as many stitches as you will need and then knitting stitches together across the first row. This is a good way to start socks. The cast-on will be sufficiently stretchy to accommodate the wider Column Pattern and the sock will slip onto the foot effortlessly.

Another good way to begin a piece of knitting is to work a strip of sideways garter stitch since it will remain stretchy. This can be used for the cuff of a sock or sweater, or to start a shawl. Once you have the same number of garter ridges as you will want stitches, pick up one stitch per garter ridge along the edge and establish the Column Pattern. The garter edging can be made in one color or in two. By alternating color A and color B every two rows in the garter strip, you can then pick up the stitches for your columns along the edge so that they will match and 'grow' out of the garter stripes.

LONG-TAIL LOOP CAST-ON

1 Hold needle in left hand and tail of yarn in right hand (allowing about 1" for each stitch to be cast on).
2 Bring right index finger under yarn, pointing toward you.

3 Turn index finger to point away from you.
4 Insert tip of needle under yarn on index finger (see above); remove finger and draw yarn snug, forming a stitch.
Repeat Steps 2–4. After every few stitches, allow the yarn to hang freely to restore its original twist.

YO BIND-OFF

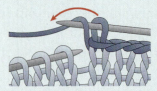

1 Knit 1 stitch as usual.
2 Yarn over.
3 With left needle, pass first stitch on right needle over the yarn-over. . .

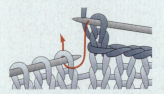

. . . and off the needle.
4 Knit 1 more stitch.
5 Pass yarn-over over this knit stitch and off the needle (one stitch bound off).

KNIT LOOP BIND-OFF

1 Insert tapestry needle into second stitch as if to knit and pull through to the back, leaving stitches on knitting needle.

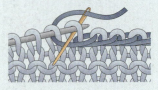

2 Insert tapestry needle into first stitch as if to purl, pull through, and drop stitch off knitting needle.

Binding off

Binding off in the k1b stitch pattern also must be loose because the stitches are so wide. A number of projects make use of the technique of inserting a yarn-over between the stitches that you are binding off. The width of this YO bind-off can be adjusted by inserting a yarn-over between every stitch or after every two or three stitches, giving you control over the amount of extra width you add to your bind-off.

Since many of the projects make use of the long-tail loop cast-on, there was a need for a corresponding bind-off. The solution here was a sewn technique, the loop bind-off, which matches the loop cast-on. It can be worked as a knit loop bind-off or as a purl loop bind-off (see *Techniques* page 138), thus precisely replicating the cast-on used at the beginning of the project.

Just as a strip of sideways garter stitch makes a good cast-on, it is also great for a matching bind-off. By working the garter ridges in alternating colors, they flow seamlessly from the top of the columns.

Correcting Mistakes

There comes a time in the life of every knitter when there is a need to pick up a dropped stitch or to rip back one or more rows. The Column Pattern calls for special attention because of the floats that lie behind the stitches. These floats are created by knitting one below, so when you go to correct your knitting, they have to be captured and reunited with the stitch they belong to.

As you rip back stitch-by-stitch, you will notice that there is an extra loop accompanying every other stitch on your needle. This extra loop is the float from the k1b or the p1b. At this point, you have two options: one is to reconstruct the stitch by pulling it over its float. As you do so, orient yourself by the fact that the stitch is the same color as the column you are working on at that moment, while the float is the other color that had dropped behind your work as it was knit or purled below. The other option is to take a shortcut: (Ripping Back, page 144) don't reconstruct the stitch. Just leave the two-loop combo on the needle as you rip back one stitch at a time. When you go to knit that row, knit the stitch together with its float, and you'll be back where you started.

Picking up dropped stitches also involves restoring the floats to their correct position. You will do this similarly to picking up dropped stitches in stockinette stitch. However, each picked up stitch in a column has to have its float secured behind. (Picking up dropped k1b stitches, page 144) Let the A and B colors guide you. Insert a crochet hook into the stitch below your dropped stitch, catch the float as well as the stitch above, and draw the new stitch through the stitch and under the float that are on the crochet hook. Check the reverse side of your work to make sure that your float is secured behind the reconstructed stitch and not just 'floating' there.

If you have dropped a stitch down quite a few rows, or if you have dropped two adjacent stitches, you might prefer to take a deep breath, thread a small needle through an intact row, take the knitting off the needle and rip back. As you replace the stitches on your needle, scoop up the float together with the stitch and you're all set.

Strip of garter stitch used as a bind-off. Note that the color of the ridge matches the color of the column.

Needles

Generally speaking, you can use the needle size recommended on the ball band of the yarn. However, it may be desirable to knit more loosely for projects such as shawls and more tightly for socks and the like. Your gauge swatch will guide you here. By and large, a good starting point for your swatch is to begin with the needle size recommended on the ball band. If you are a firm knitter, the recommended size could be just right. Loose knitters might want to go down a size since the k1b stitch pattern is a bit looser than stockinette stitch.

Since the Column Pattern involves sliding your work to the opposite end of the needle, it calls for circular or double-pointed needles. Blunt-tipped needles will enhance your knitting pleasure since they are less likely to pierce and split the yarn as you insert the needle into the stitch below.

Yarns

Any type of yarn can be used with this technique. Yarns of the same thickness and texture can be used throughout, producing a smooth fabric. For a different look, a thick yarn can be combined with a thin one, resulting in peaks and valleys of texture with a ribbed appearance. By combining a bulky yarn with a thin yarn, you can create a fabric that highlights the beautiful bulky yarn but without the heaviness typical of such yarns. The k1b technique will 'thin out' the more voluminous yarn.

Totally different types of yarn can be combined in a single project, such as a mohair yarn with a slick rayon ribbon. The Tattersall Scarf (page 118) combines a thick unplied yarn with a smooth alpaca. Novelty yarns are an especially nice touch and can be showcased with this technique by combining one skein of something fancy with several skeins of a simpler yarn.

Selvedges

The edges of your k1b project can be worked in a number of different ways, depending on the intended use. Knitting the first and last stitch on the right side and purling them on the wrong side creates little bumps along the edge, forming a firm selvedge for seaming and picking up stitches for borders and bands.

For projects where the edges will be exposed, such as scarves and afghans, you can work two or three stitches in garter stitch along the sides. This technique was used for the Inside-Outside Scarf, Laid-Back Lapels, and several other projects.

Another option is to slip the first stitch of each row (On the Easy Side sweater, page 40). The third swatch pictured here shows that slipping the first stitch creates a lovely candy-cane effect running up the side of the fabric. Once again, since the fabric tends to lie flat, such a selvedge treatment is perfectly adequate as a finish for an exposed edge.

Selvedges from top to bottom: First and last stitch knit; First and last 2 stitches worked in garter stitch; First stitch of every row slipped.

Stockinette stitch swatch superimposed on the Column Pattern. Same yarn, same needle size. What a difference k1b makes!

Color

The Column Pattern affords great latitude in the use of color. Give your imagination free rein. Inspiration can come from Shetland colorways, from the colors found in nature, or you can follow your own path. Needlepoint yarns with their many gradations offer a myriad of color possibilities. On a different note, you can stay within one color range and use two yarns that have different textures, producing a more understated effect.

Hand-painted yarns are perfect for the k1b stitch. Since every other stitch is drawn upwards from the preceding row, you are always alternating the color of adjacent stitches. By selecting a harmonizing solid yarn for the other color, you can nicely break up the streaking or pooling that sometimes occurs with such variegated yarns. You know how you sometimes fall in love with a hand-dyed skein? You are drawn to the hank of yarn, still wound into eye-catching splashes of color. And yet, when you start to knit with it, you find that it has merged into a blend of indistinct color. Or at the very least your stockinette stitch looks predictable and mottled rather than unique and multi-hued. The Column Pattern keeps those color flashes intact, keeps the artisan yarn looking the way you had visualized.

The Inside-Outside Scarf demonstrates a technique for using yarns with distinctive color changes. A long-repeat variegated yarn is worked from the inside of one ball and the outside of another. The colors of each column progress through the sequence in the opposite direction, intersect part way through the scarf, and then diverge.

Weaving

Weaving can be used to great effect with the k1b stitch to showcase a novelty yarn, to add texture, to create a plaid, to make the fabric warmer, or to stabilize it. You can make a very dramatic scarf, for example, by weaving in a small amount of ribbon. The non-stretchy ribbon will create a firm fabric. Using a bouncy yarn, on the other hand, will allow the article to remain supple. Weaving with a third yarn has been used to advantage in the Tattersall Scarf (top left, page 118), lending a complexity to what is otherwise a very simple project. The k1b stitch also provides a good foundation for creating a plaid. You can weave color A over color B columns for a more pronounced plaid, or color A over color A columns for a more subtle look. Interestingly, since you weave by just going under the two 'legs' of the stitch, the woven yarn is not visible on the wrong side because it is concealed behind the floats.

Cables

All kinds of cables can be worked in the k1b stitch, with some dramatic results. The Yin Yang cardigan (page 28) and the Cabled Socks (page 130) show the use of cables incorporated on a background of the Column Pattern. Whether you prefer crossed cables or traveling cables, the Column Pattern offers boundless options. One of the benefits of cables in the k1b stitch pattern is that the left-hand stitch of the cable does not become loose as is sometimes the case when cables are worked on a purl background.

Paired k1b stitches

Most projects in this book alternate one k1b stitch with one knit stitch, but the columns can also be worked as a two-by-two design. In the Block Sweater (the cover sweater, page 52) and the T-V Top (page 66), two k1b stitches are worked next to each other, followed by two regular knit stitches. This technique produces longer 'floats' and a looser fabric with more pronounced color groupings.

Intarsia

The k1b stitch can also be part of an intarsia project, as in the Blocks of Color blanket (page 92) and Another Facet sweater (page 56). The intarsia segments can be constructed horizontally, vertically, and diagonally. One of the nice things about the Column Pattern is that it does not form loose stitches at the color changes as often happens with intarsia worked in stockinette stitch. Since every other row is worked all the way across, the intarsia junctions remain neat and snug.

Felting

The Column Pattern lends itself very well to felted projects. The k1b fabric is thicker than regular stockinette because the floats behind the stitches add volume to the knitting. The result is a solid and sturdy, felted fabric with a lot of body.

No sewing, no weaving. A cutting-edge technique: a fringe to end all ends.

Handling yarn ends

When working with the k1b stitch, it is preferable not to weave in the tails as you go. If you do, you run the risk of not being able to work neatly into the stitch below, and the tails would make the fabric too thick. Weaving as you go also reduces the flexibility and distorts the stitch pattern of the k1b fabric.

A good approach is to join yarns at the end of the rows. Otherwise, since the stitch pattern is somewhat loose, the ends might be hard to anchor in the stitches in the middle of the fabric and could show through on the right side.

Splicing is a good option when it comes to joining a new strand of yarn. Two practical splicing methods are illustrated in the Technique section on page 144.

"To knot or not to knot, that is the question." There are two schools of thought about knotting: those who knot and those who do not knot. I am a knotter, especially when working with very smooth yarns, such as rayon or silk. Since the k1b stitch pattern is loose by nature, I prefer to err on the side of caution when it comes to knots.

If you are using many different colored yarns from your stash, you can cut each yarn at the end of each row, leaving a tail of a few inches. This way, you can slide back to the beginning of the needle so as to always work on the knit side of the piece rather than on the purl side. Instead of weaving these ends in later, you can just tie them with an overhand knot, creating a neat 'fringe.' This approach was used for the Light-to-Dark Vest (page 8), and for several pieces in the Stashbuster section, beginning on page 132. You can also use a sewing machine to make two or three rows of very small stitches to anchor the ends. The tails can then be trimmed fairly short.

K2TOGb

A right-slanting, single decrease with color A on top of the 2 color B loops.

Double increase worked at armhole of Yin Yang cardigan.

Short rows shape the Curves and Columns vest.

Reverse stockinette stitch in a contrast color finishes a front opening.

Increasing and decreasing

Increasing and decreasing call for special care when you are working with the k1b stitch. If you increase or decrease only one stitch, you will end up with two columns of the same color next to each other, which might, of course, be the desired effect. If not, working double increases and double decreases will maintain the integrity of the Column Pattern.

Because of the different ratio between stitches and rows, the number of rows between increases and decreases in the k1b stitch pattern differs from what it might be for a project worked in stockinette stitch. This difference has significant consequences when it comes to increasing and decreasing. For example, while you might increase every 4 or 6 rows along the edge of a sleeve in stockinette stitch, you would increase every 8 or 12 rows for a sweater made with the Column Pattern. V-neck shaping in stockinette stitch might call for decreases every 4th row while the decreases in the k1b variant may be distributed every 8th row.

Short rows

Short rows are very easy to work in the Column Pattern since they do not need to be wrapped and are virtually invisible. They are used to form the long slanted line along the shoulder in the Offset Tabard (page 70) and to shape the curved lower edge of the Curves and Columns vest (page 18).

Bands, borders and edgings

Since the k1b fabric is thicker than stockinette, the edge treatments used in a number of sweaters, afghans, and other items have been designed to be fairly voluminous. I have chosen these heftier edgings to match the hand of the k1b fabric rather than, for example, regular ribbing, which yields a somewhat thin fabric. Garter stitch is suitable since it is nice and thick, and its wider gauge approaches that of the Column Pattern. Sometimes a nice touch is to wrap the edges, especially if you have a lot of ends from yarns of many different colors. A band consisting of a few rows of reverse stockinette stitch is a good choice and rolls nicely around the edge (see bottom photo). You can also make a fold-over stockinette band with a purl ridge for a crisp crease and then loosely tack down the last row of live stitches on the inside.

A border can also serve as a bind-off, and that same border can then be added to the beginning of the piece by picking up stitches along the long-tail loop cast-on, so that the beginning and the end of the piece will match.

Crocheted crab stitch or single crochet is another option for edges. It wraps the edges and is nice and firm. Since the k1b pattern lies flat and does not curl, even a narrow border like a crochet edging works well. Crochet edgings are used for the Checkmark scarves (page 82) and Gossamer Square (page 78).

Pick-up ratio

The pick-up ratio will vary, depending on the yarn thickness and on where you are picking up stitches. Along the vertical edge of the Column Pattern, the pick-up is worked in the 'ditch' between the selvedge stitch and the first column. A generally useful ratio is to pick up two stitches for every three visible stitches (which actually corresponds to two stitches for every six rows). If you are using a thinner yarn for the edging, a pick-up ratio of one stitch for each visible stitch will be just right.

Along the horizontal edge of the Column Pattern, the pick-up ratio is quite different, because of the width of the stitch pattern. If you are adding an edging to the lower edge of a garment, for example, a good ratio is 1 stitch for each column; the pick-up is worked right into the 'heart' of the stitch at the base of the column. This band will be slightly snug and will hold the lower edge of the garment together like ribbing in a more conventional sweater. If your border calls for more stitches than the number of columns, you will pick up an extra stitch between columns from time to time.

Seams

There are several ways to join seams, depending on the desired effect. If the columns next to the selvedge stitch of the two pieces being joined are the same color, a mattress stitch down the middle of the column on each side of the seam will create a virtually invisible join. If the columns being joined are of opposing colors, a mattress stitch between the selvedge stitch and the first column of each piece will retain the distribution of the stripes.

Stitches can also be picked up along both sides between the selvedge stitch and the first column and then joined with a 3-needle bind-off. This technique is especially effective if the columns on each piece are in one color and the picked-up stitches and the 3-needle bind-off are in the other color since this produces another column that blends in perfectly with the Column Pattern (bottom photo).

Other uses for the k1b stitch

The k1b stitch is a handy way to eliminate the jog when working stripes in the round in knit, purl, or garter stitch: by working a k1b after the end of the first round of the new color and moving the marker one stitch to the left, you will have no jog.

Another practical use for the k1b stitch is at the end of a bind-off row. When you bind off the last stitch in a row, it is often loose. By knitting into the stitch below, you can bind off in the normal manner and that last stitch will tighten up.

Shoulders joined with 3-needle YO bind-off.

Side seam worked in 3-needle YO bind-off blends into Column Pattern.

Schematics

You will notice that, in this book, stitch counts as well as inches have been incorporated into the schematics and indicated by different colors. This puts all of the information at your fingertips with great clarity as you follow the instructions. A quick glance at the schematic, and you can check your numbers, easily keeping track of where you are in the pattern.

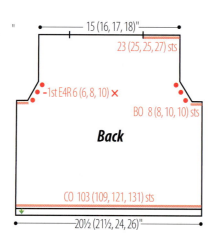

Back

15 (16, 17, 18)"

23 (25, 25, 27) sts

–1st E4R 6 (6, 8, 10) ✕

BO 8 (8, 10, 10) sts

CO 103 (109, 121, 131) sts

20½ (21½, 24, 26)"

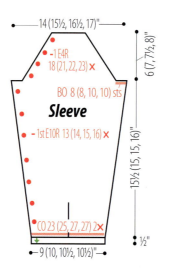

Left Front

4½ (5, 5, 5½)"

1"

–1st E4R 5 (6, 7, 8) ✕

BO 7 (8, 9, 10) sts

7 (7, 8, 9)"

15 (16, 18, 20)"

23 sts

11 (12, 13, 14)"

CO 49 (53, 59, 65) sts

½"

10 (10½, 12, 13)"

Sleeve

14 (15½, 16½, 17)"

6 (7, 7½, 8)"

–1 E4R 18 (21, 22, 23) ✕

BO 8 (8, 10, 10) sts

–1st E10R 13 (14, 15, 16) ✕

15½ (15, 15, 16)"

CO 23 (25, 27, 27) 2✕

½"

9 (10, 10½, 10½)"

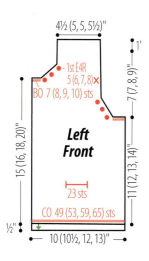

The Projects

The projects start with a simple vest that will introduce you to the k1b stitch—working with variegated yarns without having to deal with shaping—and progress to more complex garments that will enhance your skills. Along the way you will learn how to apply the k1b stitch in many novel ways. But once you have mastered knitting into the stitch below, the rest is just a variation on a theme.

In developing the projects, I devised different ways of assembling and finishing the garments—3-needle bind-offs with inserted yarn-overs, a so-called zigzag 3-needle bind-off, unexpected edgings, and more.

I hope you will have as much fun combining yarns and trying out techniques as I had in creating the projects.

1

Vests

8

Each row of the **Light-To-Dark Vest** is worked on the RS so no purl or p1b stitches are involved. As a result, the pattern repeat is a mere 2 rows, making the vest much easier than it looks.

18

Curves and Columns shows that the k1b pattern can be used for short rows. Because of the structure of the stitch pattern, it is easy: no need to wrap the stitches.

14

Sideways garter stitch trims the top of the lapel, the armhole, and the lower edge of **Laid-Back Lapels.**

12

Who says the right side is always right? In fact, there is nothing wrong with the wrong side of the column pattern! The lapels fold back and reveal the opposite face, regardless of how the **Reversible Vest** is worn.

4

Pinstripes are also a guy thing: simply pick some muted colors and make one for him.

3

Column Pattern OVER AN ODD NUMBER OF STITCHES
Row 1 (RS) With A, k1, *k1, k1b; repeat from *, end k2, slide.
Row 2 (RS) With B, k1, *k1b, k1; repeat from *, turn.
Row 3 (WS) With A, p1, *p1, p1b; repeat from *, end p2, slide.
Row 4 (WS) With B, p1, *p1b, p1; repeat from *, turn.
Repeat rows 1–4 for Column Pattern.

Column Pattern

2-st repeat

☐ K on RS, p on WS
☑ K1b on RS, p1b on WS

Color Sequence *Work 12 rows with A as Blue and B as Gray; work 12 rows with A as Gray and B as Blue; repeat from *.

Pintripes

INTERMEDIATE

STANDARD FIT **LOOSE FIT**

Size S (M, L, 1X, 2X, 3X)
Men's Size XS (S, M, L, 1X, 2X)
A 37 (40½, 43½, 47, 53½, 56)"
B 19 (20, 21, 22, 23, 24)"
21 (22, 23, 24, 25, 26)"

10cm/4"
40/40
10/14
• **over Column Pattern with larger needles**

1 2 3 **4** 5 6

Medium weight
A • 350 (375, 425, 500, 575, 625) yds
B • 300 (325, 375, 425, 500, 550) yds
A&B • 275 (325, 350, 400, 475, 525) yds each
C • 110 (120, 135, 150, 175, 200) yds

6mm/US 10/5mm/US 8, or size to obtain gauge, 60cm (24") or longer
5mm/US 8/4mm/US 6, 40cm (16") and 80cm–100cm (32–40") long

5 (5, 5, 5, 7, 7) • 16mm (5/8")

Stitch markers and stitch holders

Medium: 4 balls ELSEBETH LAVOLD Angora in Burgundy Red (A) and 2 balls NORO Kochoran in color 17 Magenta (B)
Large: 5 balls each FILATURA DI CROSA Zara Plus in 10 Midnight Blue and 29 Charcoal Gray ; 2 balls 14 Brown (C)

Notes

1 See *Techniques*, page 138, for long-tail loop cast-on, k1b, p1b, k2tog, SSK, M1, slide, YO bind-off, 3-needle YO bind-off, YO buttonhole, and pick up stitches. *2* Work edge stitches firmly (see page 120, Note 3). *3* Numbers for the Woman's vest appear first (in red) and for the Man's vest second (in blue). Shared numbers appear in black. *4* For Man's vest in Offset Column Pattern as shown on page 6, work in Column Pattern following Color Sequence.

VEST

With larger needle and A (Blue) and using long-tail loop cast-on, cast on 93 (101, 109, 117, 133, 141) 129 (141, 153, 165, 189, 197) stitches. Join B (Gray) at tail-end of needle and purl across row (A and B are now at same end of needle); turn. Work Column Pattern until piece measures approximately 11½ (12, 12½, 13, 13½, 14)" 13½ (14, 14½, 15, 15½, 16)", end with a RS A row (row 1 of pattern).
Divide for fronts and back: Next row (RS B row) Work 19 (21, 23, 25, 27, 29) 26 (30, 34, 35, 40, 42) stitches and place on hold for right front, work 7 (7, 7, 7, 11, 11) 11 (11, 11, 13, 15, 15) stitches and place on hold for right underarm, work 41 (45, 49, 53, 57, 61) 55 (59, 63, 69, 79, 83) stitches and place on hold for back, work 7 (7, 7, 7, 11, 11) 11 (11, 11, 13, 15, 15) stitches and place on hold for left underarm, work 19 (21, 23, 25, 27, 29) 26 (30, 34, 35, 40, 42) stitches (left front).

Left front

Work 2 rows even.
Shape armhole and V-neck
K2tog at beginning of every RS A row 4 (4, 4, 6, 6, 6) 5 (5, 5, 6, 8, 7) times for armhole, AT SAME TIME, SSK at end of every RS A row 6 (7, 12, 7, 8, 8) times, then every other RS A row 7 (8, 8, 8, 9, 9) 5 (6, 4, 7, 7, 8) times for neck—8 (9, 11, 11, 12, 14) 10 (12, 13, 15, 17, 19) stitches remain. Work even until piece measures approximately 19 (20, 21, 22, 23, 24)" 21 (22, 23, 24, 25, 26)", end with a RS B row. Place stitches on hold.

Back

Place 41 (45, 49, 53, 57, 61) 55 (59, 63, 69, 79, 83) stitches of back on needle. With WS facing, join A and B. Work 2 rows even.
Shape armholes
K2tog at beginning and SSK at end of every RS A row 4 (4, 4, 6, 6, 6) 5 (5, 5, 6, 8, 7) times—33 (37, 41, 41, 45, 49) 45 (49, 53, 57, 63, 69) stitches remain. Work even until piece measures same length as left front. Place stitches on hold.

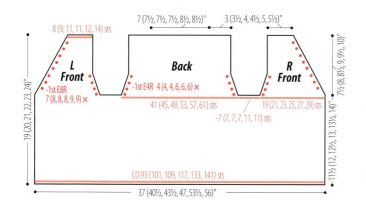

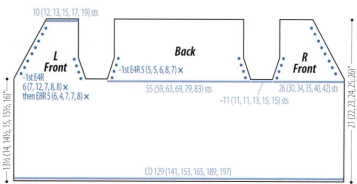

Right front

Place 19 (21, 23, 25, 27, 29) 26 (30, 34, 35, 40, 42) stitches of right front on needle. With WS facing, join A and B at armhole. Work as for left front EXCEPT SSK at end of every RS A row 4 (4, 4, 6, 6, 6) 5 (5, 5, 6, 8, 7) times for armhole and k2tog at beginning of every RS A row 6 (7, 12, 7, 8, 8) times, then every other RS A row 7 (8, 8, 8, 9, 9) 5 (6, 4, 7, 7, 8) times for neck. Leave stitches on needle. Do not cut B.

Join shoulders

With WS together and B, work 3-needle YO bind-off to join the 8 (9, 11, 11, 12, 14) 10 (12, 13, 15, 17, 19) stitches of right shoulders, continue across back of neck with YO bind-off until 8 (9, 11, 11, 12, 14) 10 (12, 13, 15, 17, 19) stitches remain. Join left shoulders with 3-needle YO bind-off.

Finishing

Front/back button band With RS facing, smaller 32" needle, and A (C), begin at right shoulder, and pick up and knit 1 stitch in each column across back neck and 1 stitch for each V along left front, place corner marker, 3 stitches for every 2 columns along lower edge (1 stitch in a V, 1 stitch between Vs, and 1 stitch in next V), place corner marker, 1 stitch for each V along right front. Place beginning-of-round marker and join.

Round 1 Purl. ***Round 2*** [Purl to 1 stitch before corner marker, M1, p1, slip marker, p1, M1] 2 times, purl to end of round. ***Round 3*** Knit, making 5 (5, 5, 5, 7, 7) YO buttonholes evenly spaced along right front (left front), working top buttonhole at the base of V-neck shaping and bottom buttonhole 2 stitches above marker at lower corner. ***Round 4*** [Knit to 1 stitch before corner marker, M1, k1, slip marker, k1, M1] 2 times, knit to end of round. ***Round 5*** Purl. ***Round 6*** [Purl to 2 stitches before corner marker, p2tog, slip marker, p2tog] 2 times, purl to end of round. Bind off purlwise.

Armhole bands

With RS facing, smaller 16" circular needle, and A (C), knit 7 (7, 7, 7, 11, 11) 11 (11, 11, 13, 15, 15) stitches on hold at armhole, pick up and knit 1 stitch for each column along diagonal edge and 1 stitch for each V along straight edge. Place marker and join. Purl 2 rounds, knit 2 rounds, purl 2 rounds. Bind off purlwise.

Finishing

Sew buttons onto front opposite buttonholes.

The long-tail loop cast-on adds minimal bulk and disappears discretely behind the stitches that are picked up for the border.

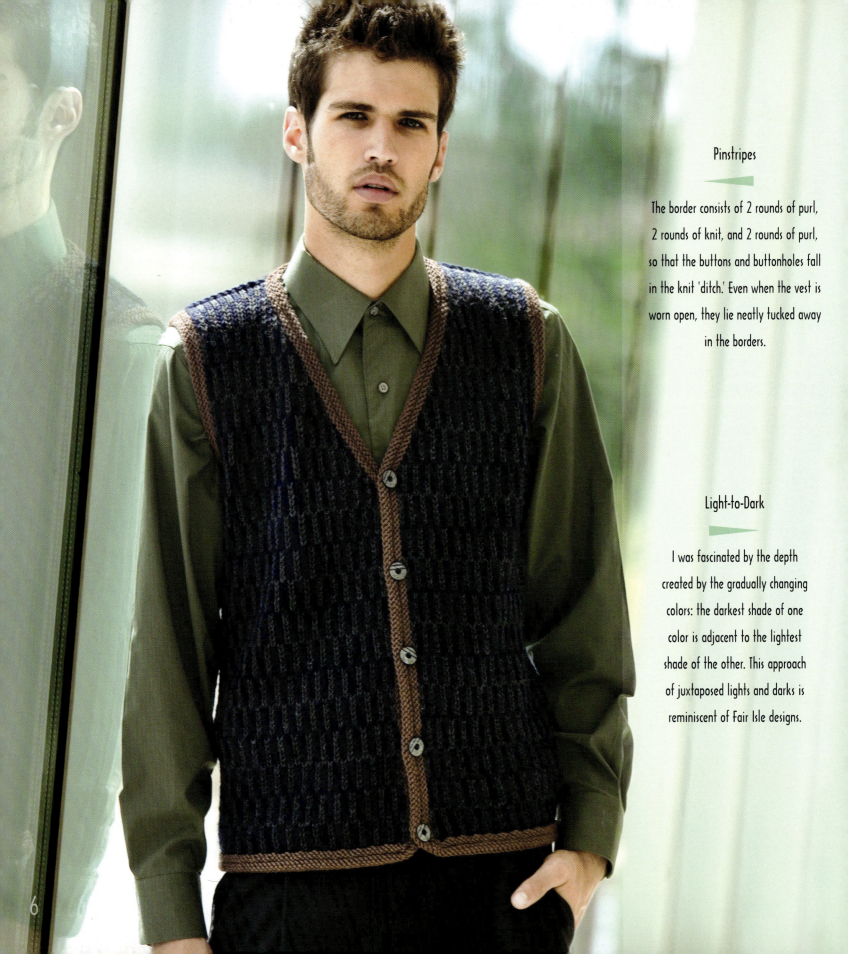

Pinstripes

The border consists of 2 rounds of purl, 2 rounds of knit, and 2 rounds of purl, so that the buttons and buttonholes fall in the knit 'ditch.' Even when the vest is worn open, they lie neatly tucked away in the borders.

Light-to-Dark

I was fascinated by the depth created by the gradually changing colors: the darkest shade of one color is adjacent to the lightest shade of the other. This approach of juxtaposed lights and darks is reminiscent of Fair Isle designs.

Fringed Column Pattern OVER AN ODD NUMBER OF STITCHES

Note Leave a tail of 2" at the beginning and end of each row.

Row 1 (RS) With A, k1, *k1b, k1; repeat from *, cut yarn, slide.

Row 2 (RS) With B, k1, *k1, k1b; repeat from *, end k2, cut yarn, slide.

Tighten edge stitches as you tie A and B ends together with an overhand knot.

Repeat rows 1–2 for Fringed Column Pattern.

Fringed Column Pattern

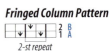

2-st repeat

☐ Knit
▾ K1b

Light-to-Dark Vest

Notes

1 See *Techniques*, page 138, for long-tail loop cast-on, k1b, M1, overhand knot, k2tog, SSK, YO bind-off, 3-needle YO bind-off, YO buttonhole, splicing, and slide. *2* Work with RS facing on all rows. *3* Do not join yarn in middle of row. Splice shorter lengths together or use for shorter rows at top of vest.

Body

With larger needle and A1 and using long-tail loop cast-on, cast on 129 (137, 153, 169, 185) stitches, cut yarn, slide. Join B6 at tail-end of needle and knit across row (A1 and B6 are now at same end of needle); cut both yarns leaving 2" tails, slide. Work in Column Pattern following Color Sequence and cutting yarn at end of every row until piece measures approximately 10½ (11, 11½ , 12, 12½)" from beginning, end with a B row (row 2 of pattern).

Divide for fronts and back: Next row (A row) Work 29 (31, 33, 37, 39) stitches and place on hold for right front, work 7 (7, 11, 11, 15) stitches and place on hold for right underarm, work 57 (61, 65, 73, 77) stitches and place on hold for back, work 7 (7, 11, 11, 15) stitches and place on hold for left underarm, work 29 (31, 33, 37, 39) stitches (left front).

Left front

Work 3 rows.

Shape armhole and V-neck

K2tog at beginning of every other A row 6 (6, 6, 8, 8) times for armhole, AT SAME TIME, SSK at end of every 4th A row 11(12, 13, 14, 14) times for neck. Work even until piece measures approximately 20 (21, 22, 23, 24)", end with a B row. Place stitches on hold.

Back

Place 57 (61, 65, 73, 77) stitches of back on larger needle. Work 3 rows.

Shape armholes

K2tog at beginning and SSK at end of every other RS A row 6 (6, 6, 8, 8) times—45 (49, 53, 57, 61) stitches remain. Work even until piece measures same length as left front. Place stitches on hold.

Right front

Place 29 (31, 33, 37, 39) stitches of right front on larger needle. Work as for left front EXCEPT k2tog at beginning of every 4th RS row 11(12, 13, 14, 14) times for neck and SSK at end of every other A row 6 (6, 6, 8, 8) times for armhole. Leave stitches on needle. Do not cut B.

INTERMEDIATE

STANDARD FIT

S (M, L, 1X, 2X)

A 37 (39½, 44, 48½, 53)"
B 21 (22, 23, 24, 25)"

10cm/4"

44

14

• over Column Pattern
with larger needle

1 2 **3** 4 5 6

Light weight

A1, A6, B1, B6 • 33 (40, 45, 50, 55) yds each
A2, A3, A5, B2, B3, B5 • 66 (75, 85, 95, 110) yds each
A4, B4 • 110 (125, 145, 160, 180) yds each

4mm/US 6, or size to obtain gauge, 60cm (24") or longer
3.5mm/US 4, 40cm (16") and 80–100cm (32–40") long

7 (7, 7, 8, 8) • 16mm (5/8")

&

Stitch holders and yarn needle

Small: 3 skeins each ANCHOR Tapisserie Wool-Laine 8542 (A1, lightest purple), 8552 (A6, darkest purple), 9674 (B1, lightest beige), 9684 (B6, darkest beige); 6 skeins each 8544 (A2), 8546 (A3), 8550 (A5), 9676 (B2), 9678 (B3), 9682 (B5); 10 skeins each 8548 (A4), 9680 (B4)

Color Sequence 20-ROW REPEAT

As you work Column Pattern, change color for each row as follows A1, B6, A2, B5, A3, B4, A4, B3, A5, B2, A6, B1, A5, B2, A4, B3, A3, B4, A2, B5; repeat from *.

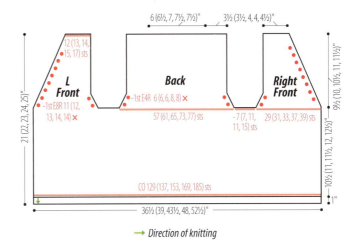

6 (6½, 7, 7½, 7½)"   3½ (3½, 4, 4, 4½)"

L Front
12 (13, 14, 15, 17) sts

Back
-1st E4R 6 (6, 6, 8, 8) ✕

Right Front

-1st E8R 11 (12, 13, 14, 14) ✕

57 (61, 65, 73, 77) sts

-7 (7, 11, 11, 15) sts   29 (31, 33, 37, 39) sts

21 (22, 23, 24, 25)"

9½ (10, 10½, 11, 11½)"

10½ (11, 11½, 12, 12½)"

CO 129 (137, 153, 169, 185) sts

1"

36½ (39, 43½, 48, 52½)"

→ *Direction of knitting*

Join shoulders

With WS together and B, work 3-needle YO bind-off to join the 12 (13, 14, 15, 17) stitches of right shoulders, continue across back of neck with YO bind-off until 12 (13, 14, 15, 17) stitches remain. Join left shoulders with 3-needle YO bind-off.

Finishing

Trim fringe ends to 1". Block.

Front/Back button band With RS facing and smaller 32–40" needle and A4, begin at right shoulder and pick up and knit 1 stitch in each column across back neck and 2 stitches for every 3 Vs along left front, place corner marker, 1 stitch for each column along lower edge, place corner marker, 2 stitches for every 3 Vs along right front. Place beginning-of-round marker and join. Purl 1 round with B4. **Increase round** With A4, *purl to 1 stitch before corner marker, M1, p1, slip marker, p1, M1, repeat from *, purl to end of round. **Buttonhole round** With B4, knit to second corner marker. Work 7 (7, 7, 8, 8) YO buttonholes evenly spaced along right front edge, working first buttonhole 2 stitches past marker and last buttonhole at beginning of V-neck shaping, knit to end of round. **Increase round** With A4, *knit to 1 stitch before corner marker, M1, k1, slip marker, k1, M1, repeat from *, knit to end of round. Purl 1 round with B4 and 1 round with A4. With B4 and larger needle, bind off very loosely purlwise.

Armhole bands With RS facing, smaller 16" needle and A4, knit 7 (7, 11, 11, 15) stitches on hold at underarm, pick up and knit 2 stitches for every 3 Vs along diagonal and straight edges. Place marker and join. Alternating 1 round of B4 and 1 round of A4, purl 2 rounds, knit 2 rounds, purl 2 rounds. With B4 and larger needle, bind off very loosely purlwise. Sew buttons on left front band to correspond to buttonholes.

TIP To hold and organize yarns, place yarns in 6 small zipper bags. You could label them A1, B1; A2, B2; etc. Or put the lightest A with the darkest B, etc., grouping the colors the way they will be worked: A1 and B6 labeled 1st bag; A2 and B5 labeled 2nd bag; A3 and B4 labeled 3rd bag; A4 and B3 labeled 4th bag; A5 and B2 labeled 5th bag; A6 and B1 labeled 6th bag. Then it is easy to work through the bags in 1-2-3-4-5-6-5-4-3-2-1 order.

The knotted ends create a decorative fringe that flips neatly to the inside when the stitches are picked up for the borders.

The selvedge stitch is knit on every row, creating the colorful stockinette stitch edge that can be seen next to the overhand knots. The border is picked up between the selvedge stitch and the first column.

Reversible Vests

Different gauge – different appearance. From a casual look with jeans to an elegant wrap in fancy yarn. The fronts overlap slightly and can be fastened or folded back to swing freely

Although the vest has straight lines, the placement of your shawl pin will allow you to wear this garment in a flattering A-lined shape.

Column Pattern with Garter Edge OVER AN ODD NUMBER OF STITCHES

Row 1 (RS) With A, k2, * k1b, k1; repeat from *, end k1b, k2, slide.
Row 2 (RS) With B, p2, *k1, k1b; repeat from *, end k1, p2, turn.
Row 3 (WS) With A, p2, * p1b, p1; repeat from *, end p1b, p2, slide.
Row 4 (WS) With B, k2, *p1, p1b; repeat from *, end p1, k2, turn.
Repeat rows 1–4 for Column Pattern.

Reversible Vest

Notes

1 See *Techniques*, page 138, for double loop cast-on, k1b, p1b, k2tog, SSK, YO bind-off, 3-needle YO bind-off, p2tog bind-off, slide, and splicing. *2* Work the 2 garter stitches firmly. After working the first stitch of rows 1 and 3 with color A, insert needle into next stitch, then give color B a little tug before completing the stitch with A. *3* Numbers for the casual vest appear first (in red) and for the dressy vest second (in blue). Shared numbers appear in black.

Vest

With A and using double loop cast-on, cast on 109 (121, 133, 145, 157, 169) 129 (143, 157, 171, 185, 199) stitches, turn. With B, estimate a long tail as you did for A, fold yarn and knit the first stitch, bringing loop through double half-hitch. Holding the tail and working yarn together, knit across row with doubled yarn (A and B are now at same end of needle), turn. Cut long tails and continue with single strand of A and of B. With A, knit 1 row, slide. Work Column Pattern, starting with row 2, until piece measures approximately 10½ (11, 11½, 12, 12½, 13)", end with a RS A row (row 1 of pattern).

Divide for fronts and back: Next row (RS B row) Work 25 (27, 29, 31, 33, 35) 31 (33, 35, 37, 39, 41) stitches and place on hold for right front, p2tog bind off 9 (11, 13, 15, 17, 19) 11 (13, 15, 17, 19, 21) stitches for right underarm, work 41 (45, 49, 53, 57, 61) 45 (51, 57, 63, 69, 75) stitches and place on hold for back, p2tog bind off 9 (11, 13, 15, 17, 19) 11 (13, 15, 17, 19, 21) stitches for left underarm, work 25 (27, 29, 31, 33, 35) 31 (33, 35, 37, 39, 41) stitches (left front).

Left front

Next row (WS A row) Work to last 2 stitches, p2 (establishing a garter-stitch edge along armhole). Work even until piece measures approximately 19 (20, 21, 22, 23, 24)", end with a WS A row.
Next row With B and WS facing, p2tog bind off 14 (15, 16, 17, 17, 17) 18 (19, 20, 20, 20, 20) stitches, work to end of row. Place remaining 11 (12, 13, 14, 16, 18) 13 (14, 15, 17, 19, 21) stitches on hold.

Back

Place 41 (45, 49, 53, 57, 61) 45 (51, 57, 63, 69, 75) stitches of back on needle. With WS facing, join A and B.
Next row (WS A row) P2, work in pattern to last 2 stitches, p2 (establishing garter-stitch edge along each armhole). Work until piece measures same length as left front. Place stitches on hold.

EASY+

STANDARD FIT

S (M, L, 1X, 2X, 3X)
A 36 (40, 44, 48, 52, 56)"
B 19 (20, 21, 22, 23, 24)"

10cm/4"
32/42
12/14
• over Column Pattern

1 2 3 4 **5** 6
Bulky weight
A & B • 275 (325, 375, 425, 500, 550) yds each
A • 275 (325, 375, 425, 500, 550) yds each

1 2 3 **4** 5 6
Medium weight
B • 275 (325, 375, 425, 500, 550) yds each

5mm/US 8 4mm/US 6, or size to obtain gauge,
60 cm (24") or longer
Extra needle for 3-needle bind-off

&
Stitch holders, stitch markers, tapestry needle

Medium: 2 skeins each MANOS DEL URUGUAY Wool Clasica in color 106 (A) and color (B)
Small: 2 skeins each GREAT ADIRONDACK Apollo in color Tourmaline (A) Wool Crêpe in color Tourmaline (B)

Garter-stitch edge

Row 1 (RS) K2.
Row 2 (RS) P2.
Row 3 (WS) P2.
Row 4 (WS) K2.
Repeat rows 1–4 for
Garter-stitch edge.

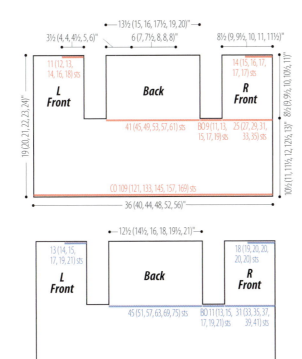

Right front

Place 25 (27, 29, 31, 33, 35) 31 (33, 35, 37, 39, 41) stitches of right front on needle. With WS facing, join A and B at armhole. Work as for left front, end with WS A row. Cut A.

Next row (WS B row) Work 11 (12, 13, 14, 16, 18) 13 (14, 15, 17, 19, 21) stitches in pattern, p2tog bind off 14 (15, 16, 17, 17, 17) 18 (19, 20, 20, 20, 20) stitches. Leave 11 (12, 13, 14, 16, 18) 13 (14, 15, 17, 19, 21) stitches on needle.

Join shoulders

With WS together and A, work 3-needle YO bind-off to join the 11 (12, 13, 14, 16, 18) 13 (14, 15, 17, 19, 21) stitches of right shoulders; slip stitch remaining from shoulder bind-off to left needle and p2tog bind off across back neck until 11 (12, 13, 14, 16, 18) 13 (14, 15, 17, 19, 21) stitches remain. Join left shoulders with 3-needle YO bind-off.

Finishing

Sew in ends so that they do not show on either side.

This is one of the easiest projects in the book since it does not require shaping, finishing, or buttonholes. The built-in garter stitch edging looks the same on both sides of the garment.

Splice your yarn as you go; you will have no ends to sew in and the vest will be reversible.

Column Pattern OVER AN ODD NUMBER OF STITCHES

Row 1 (RS) With A, k1, *k1b, k1; repeat from *, slide.
Row 2 (RS) With B, k1, * k1, k1b; repeat from *, end k2, turn.
Row 3 (WS) With A, p1, *p1b, p1; repeat from *, slide.
Row 4 (WS) With B, p1, *p1, p1b; repeat from *, end p2, turn.
Repeat rows 1–4 for Column Pattern.

Column Pattern

2-st repeat

☐ Knit on RS, purl on WS
↓ K1b on RS, p1b on WS

Laid-Back Lapels

EASY+

STANDARD FIT

S (M–L, 1X, 2X)
A 36 (42, 47, 52)"
B 20 (21, 22, 23)"

10cm/4"
32
12
• over Column Pattern

1 2 3 **4** 5 6

Medium weight
A • 225 (275, 325, 375) yds
B • 200 (250, 300, 350) yds

5mm/US 8, or size to obtain
gauge, 40cm (16") and 60cm (24")
or longer
Extra needle for 3-needle bind-off

2 • 31mm (1¼") (Optional)

Stitch holders and tapestry needle

Small: 2 skeins each MANOS DEL
URUGUAY Wool Clasica in colors
Wildflowers 113 (A) and Marl 42 (B)

Notes
1 *See Techniques*, page 138, for long-tail loop cast-on, cable cast-on, loop cast-on, k2tog, SSK, k1b, p1b, 3-needle YO bind-off, YO bind-off, graft, and slide. **2** Garter-stitch edge is worked in three variations: 1-stitch border along the top of the lapel, 2-stitch edge along armhole and front opening, and a 3-stitch band at the lower edge. **3** Work the garter-stitch edge firmly. After working the first stitch of rows 1 and 3 with color A, insert needle into next stitch, then give B a little tug before completing the stitch with A.

Back
With A and using long-tail loop cast-on, cast on 55 (63, 71, 79) stitches. Join B at tail-end of needle and purl across row (A and B are at same end of needle), turn. Work Column Pattern until piece measures approximately 10 (10½, 11, 11½)" from beginning, or desired length to underarm, end with a RS A row (row 1 of pattern).
Shape armholes
Using YO bind-off, bind off 4 (4, 6, 8) stitches at beginning of next 2 B rows—47 (55, 59, 63) stitches. K2tog at beginning and SSK at end of every RS B row 4 times—39 (47, 51, 55) stitches. Work even until armhole measures approximately 9 (9½, 10, 10½)", end with a RS A row. Place stitches on hold.

Front
Work as for back until armhole measures approximately 3 (3½, 4, 4½)", end with a WS B row.
Left front neck
Begin garter edge: Next row (RS A row) Work 18 (22, 24, 26) stitches in pattern, place marker, k2 (establishing a garter-stitch edge); place remaining stitches on hold for right front, slide.
Work in Column Pattern with garter-stitch edge until 2 rows less than back, end with a WS A row.
Lapel border With B and using loop cast-on, cast 1 stitch onto left needle. **Row 1** (WS) P2tog (border stitch together with left front stitch), turn. **Row 2** (RS) P1, turn. Repeat rows 1–2 eight (nine, ten, eleven) more times, work row 1 but do not turn, complete row in Column Pattern and place 10 (13, 14, 15) remaining stitches on hold.
Right front neck
Place 19 (23, 25, 27) stitches of right front on needle.
Begin garter border: Next row (RS A row) Join A and pick up a stitch by working into the center front stitch, k1, place marker, work 18 (22, 24, 26) stitches in pattern, slide—20 (24, 26, 28) stitches.
Work as for left front EXCEPT 2 garter stitches are at beginning of RS rows and end of WS rows AND row 1 of lapel

Garter-stitch edge

Row 1 (RS) K2.
Row 2 (RS) P2.
Row 3 (WS) P2.
Row 4 (WS) K2.
Repeat rows 1–4 for
Garter stitch edge.

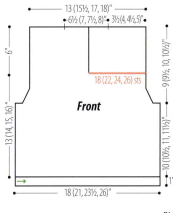

Front measurements:
13 (15½, 17, 18)"
6½ (7, 7½, 8)"
3½ (4, 4½, 5)"
6"
9 (9½, 10, 10½)"
13 (14, 15, 16)"
18 (22, 24, 26) sts
10 (10½, 11, 11½)"
1"
18 (21, 23½, 26)"

Back measurements:
10 (13, 14, 15) sts
1st E4R 4×
BO 4 (4, 6, 8) sts
CO 55 (63, 71, 79) sts

→ Direction of knitting

border is a RS row. Do not place stitches on hold. Do not cut A.

Join shoulders

With WS together and A, work 3-needle YO bind-off to join 10 (13, 14, 15) stitches of right shoulder, continue across back of neck with YO bind-off until 10 (13, 14, 15) stitches remain. Join left shoulders with 3-needle YO bind-off.

Finishing

Side seams With RS facing and B, pick up and knit 1 stitch for every V along left edge of front; with a second needle, pick up and knit the same number of stitches along right edge of back. With WS together, join with 3-needle YO bind-off. Repeat for left edge of back and right edge of front.

Armhole bands With RS facing, 16" circular needle and A, and beginning at underarm, pick up and knit 2 stitches for every 3 Vs around armhole. Join. Purl one round. With cable cast-on, cast 2 stitches onto left needle. **Row 1** (RS) P1, p2tog (last border stitch together with armhole stitch). **Row 2** (WS) P2. Repeat rows 1–2 around armhole. Graft last 2 stitches to cast-on stitches. Repeat for other armhole.

Lower band With RS facing, A, and beginning at a side seam, pick up and knit 1 stitch for each column. Join and work as for armhole band EXCEPT cable cast-on **3** stitches, p**2**, p2tog on **RS** rows, and p**3** on WS rows. Graft last **3** stitches to cast-on stitches.

Optional buttons Turn back lapels and sew a button on each.

sts   sts
sts   sts

When you pick up stitches, check that the number of stitches picked up for the *right side seam* matches the number picked up for the *left side seam*, and that the number picked up for the *left armhole* matches the *right armhole*.

The underarm bind-off has to be worked on the RS and WS color B rows. If you were to work the bind-off with color A, when you slide back to the beginning of the needle to continue with the B yarn, the B yarn would be at the edge of your work, isolated with no place to go. It would be 'stranded'— and not in the Fair Isle sense of the word. . .

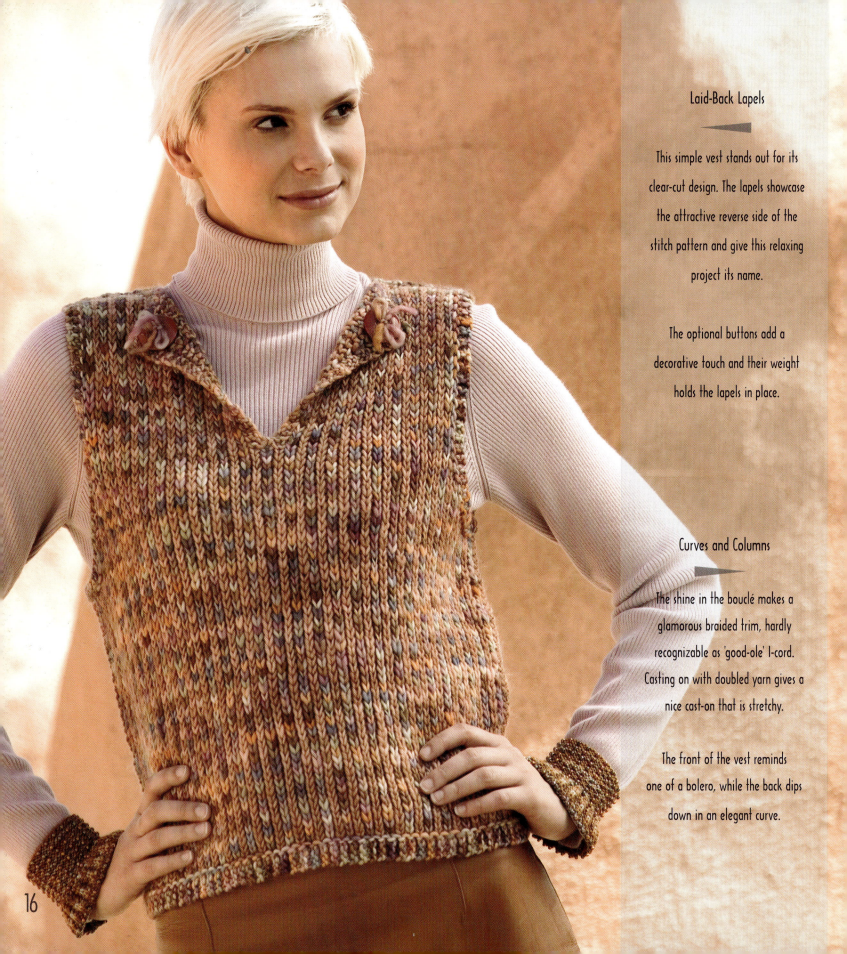

Laid-Back Lapels

This simple vest stands out for its clear-cut design. The lapels showcase the attractive reverse side of the stitch pattern and give this relaxing project its name.

The optional buttons add a decorative touch and their weight holds the lapels in place.

Curves and Columns

The shine in the bouclé makes a glamorous braided trim, hardly recognizable as 'good-ole' I-cord. Casting on with doubled yarn gives a nice cast-on that is stretchy.

The front of the vest reminds one of a bolero, while the back dips down in an elegant curve.

Column Pattern OVER AN ODD NUMBER OF STITCHES
Row 1 (RS) With A, k1, *k1b, k1; repeat from *, slide.
Row 2 (RS) With B, k1, *k1, k1b; repeat from *, end k2, turn.
Row 3 (WS) With A, p1, *p1b, p1; repeat from *, slide.
Row 4 (WS) With B, p1, *p1, p1b; repeat from *, end p2, turn.
Repeat rows 1–4 for Column Pattern.

Column Pattern
2-st repeat

☐ K on RS, p on WS
⊽ K1b on RS, p1b on WS
Ⅴ Slip purl-wise

I-cord edging Loop cast on 3 stitches, *k2, k2tog (I-cord stitch together with edging stitch), slip stitches back to left needle; repeat from *.

Curves and Columns

Notes
1 See *Techniques*, page 138, for double loop cast-on, k1b, p1b, k2tog, SSK, I-cord, and slide. *2* There is no need to wrap stitches or twist the yarns at short-row turns. Any gaps will close when subsequent rows are worked. *3* Beginning with Row 3, a second needle will be used to work short-row shaping, leaving the first needle holding stitches to be worked as the short rows lengthen.

Vest
With B, longer circular needle, and using double loop cast-on, cast on 121 (137, 153, 169) stitches. Cut long tail and continue with single strand of B; purl 2 rows. Place markers before and after the center 9 stitches.
Short-row section
Row 1 (RS A row) Work in Column Pattern to second marker, slip these 65 (73, 81, 89) stitches back to left needle.
Row 2 (RS B row) Work to second marker, turn.
Row 3 (WS A row) With second longer circular needle, slip 1 purlwise (sl 1), work **8** stitches, slide.
Row 4 (WS B row) Sl 1, work **8** stitches, turn.
Row 5 (RS A row) Sl 1, work **8** stitches, plus 4 stitches from hold needle (12 stitches), slide.
Row 6 (RS B row) Sl 1, work **12** stitches, turn.
Row 7 (WS A row) Sl 1, work **12** stitches, plus 4 stitches from hold needle (16 stitches), slide.
Row 8 (WS B row) Sl 1, work **16** stitches, turn.
Repeat rows 5–8, working 4 more stitches from hold needle to the left or right each time: **rows 9 and 10** work **20** stitches; **rows 11 and 12**, work **24** stitches. Continue in this manner until all of the hold stitches have been worked; continue with a single needle.
Work over all stitches until center front measures approximately 8 (8½, 9, 9½)" from beginning, end with a RS A row (row 1 of Column Pattern).
Divide for fronts and back: Next row (RS B row) Work 27 (31, 33, 37) stitches and place on hold for right front, work 7 (7, 11, 11) and place on hold for right underarm, work 53 (61, 65, 73) stitches and place on hold for back, work 7 (7, 11, 11) stitches and place on hold for left underarm, work 27 (31, 33, 37) stitches (left front).

Left front
Work 2 rows even.
Shape V-neck and armhole
K2tog at beginning of every RS A row 4 (4, 6, 6) times for armhole, AT SAME TIME, SSK at end of every other RS A row 10 (12, 12, 12) times for neck—13 (15, 15, 19) stitches remain. Work even until armhole measures approximately 8½ (9, 9½, 10)", end with a RS B row. Place stitches on hold.

INTERMEDIATE

STANDARD FIT

S (M/L, 1X, 2X)
A 37 (42, 47, 52)"
B 22 (23¾, 25½, 27½)"
(at center back)

10cm/4"

42
13
• over Column Pattern

1 2 3 **4** 5 6
Medium weight
A • 200 (250, 300, 350) yds
B • 300 (375, 450, 525) yds

4mm/US 6, or size to obtain gauge, two 60cm (24") or longer, and one 40cm (16")

Large decorative button

Stitch holders, yarn needle, needle & thread

Small: 2 skeins each FIESTA Watermark in color Painted Desert 15120 (A) and Socorro in color Painted Desert 27120 (B)

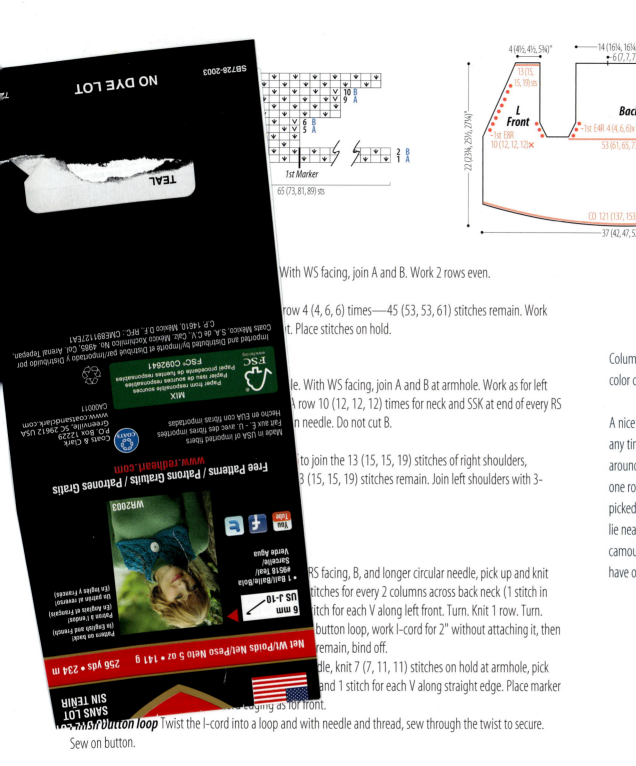

The schematic diagram (right side):

- 4 (4½, 4½, 5¾)"
- 14 (16¼, 16¼, 18¾)"
- 6 (7, 7, 7)"
- 13 (15, 15, 19) sts
- **L Front**
- **Back**
- **R Front**
- –1st E8R
- 10 (12, 12, 12)x
- –1st E4R 4 (4, 6, 6)x
- 53 (61, 65, 73) sts
- –7 (7, 11, 11) sts
- 27 (31, 33, 37) sts
- 22 (23¾, 25½, 27¼)"
- 8½ (9, 9½, 10)"
- 8 (8¼, 9, 7¾)"
- 5½ (6¼, 7, 7¾)"
- CO 121 (137, 153, 169) sts
- 37 (42, 47, 52)"

Chart: 1st Marker — 65 (73, 81, 89) sts — rows 1, 2, 5, 6, 9, 10 (A / B)

With WS facing, join A and B. Work 2 rows even.

…row 4 (4, 6, 6) times—45 (53, 53, 61) stitches remain. Work …t. Place stitches on hold.

…le. With WS facing, join A and B at armhole. Work as for left …A row 10 (12, 12, 12) times for neck and SSK at end of every RS …n needle. Do not cut B.

…l to join the 13 (15, 15, 19) stitches of right shoulders, …3 (15, 15, 19) stitches remain. Join left shoulders with 3-

…RS facing, B, and longer circular needle, pick up and knit …titches for every 2 columns across back neck (1 stitch in …tch for each V along left front. Turn. Knit 1 row. Turn. …button loop, work I-cord for 2" without attaching it, then …remain, bind off.

…dle, knit 7 (7, 11, 11) stitches on hold at armhole, pick …and 1 stitch for each V along straight edge. Place marker …edging as for front.

…*button loop* Twist the I-cord into a loop and with needle and thread, sew through the twist to secure. Sew on button.

Columns of texture rather than columns of color characterize this fabric.

A nice finishing touch that can be used any time you are picking up stitches around a neckline or armhole is to work one round of purl stitches after you have picked up the stitches. The purl bumps lie neatly over the picked-up edge, camouflaging any irregularities that might have occurred.

BOOKS

19

Jackets & Cardigans

28

K1b cables provide an exciting way to crisscross the columns: the **Yin Yang** cardigan's positive and negative 3-stitch cables.

36

Six same-sized rectangles make the **East Meets West** jacket, making this garment especially well-suited for yarn with long color changes.

26

The special bind-off used for the **Parisienne** jacket's garter edging gives the necessary flexibility and creates a substantial and attractive bind-off.

22

The fixed intervals of the Fibonacci sequence contrast with the random distribution of the colors within the light and dark groups. You pick what to work next, making every **Fibonacci Cardi-Vest** unique.

Column Pattern OVER AN ODD NUMBER OF STITCHES
Row 1 (RS) With A, k1, *k1, k1b; repeat from *, end k2, slide.
Row 2 (RS) With B, k1, *k1b, k1; repeat from *, turn.
Row 3 (WS) With A, p1, *p1, p1b; repeat from *, end p2, slide.
Row 4 (WS) With B, p1, *p1b, p1; repeat from *, turn.
Repeat rows 1–4 for Column Pattern.

Column Pattern

2-st repeat

☐ K on RS, p on WS
⬇ K1b on RS, p1b on WS

INTERMEDIATE

STANDARD FIT

Men's S (M, L, 1X, 2X)
A 36½ (41, 46, 50½, 55)"
B 23½ (24, 25, 26, 26½)"
C 32 (33, 34, 35, 36)"

10cm/4"
44
14
• over Column Pattern

1 2 3 **4** 5 6

Medium weight
6 Dark A Colors • 110 (120, 135,
150, 165) yds each
7 Light B Colors • 110 (120, 135,
150, 165) yds each

4mm/US 7, or size to obtain gauge,
60 cm (24") or longer
Needle a size or 2 smaller for armband
Extra needle for 3-needle bind-off

4mm/US 7

7 (7, 8, 9, 9) • 19mm (¾") for front
12 (13, 13, 14, 14) • 15mm (½")
for sleeves

Stitch markers, stitch holders, and
yarn needle

Medium: 1 ball each ROWAN Scottish
Tweed DK in *Dark A Colors:* 23 Midnight,
22 Celtic Mix, 16 Thistle, 31 Indigo,
19 Peat, 17 Lobster
Light B Colors: 07 Lewis Grey, 08 Herring,
04 Stormy Grey, 15 Apple, 018 Thatch,
29 Autumn, 30 Purple Heather

Fibonacci Cardi-Vest

Notes
1 See *Techniques*, page 138, for long-tail loop cast-on, k1b, p1b, double increase, k2tog, SSK, YO buttonhole, 3-needle YO bind-off, YO bind-off, p2tog bind-off, and slide. *2* Change yarns at edges, leaving 3" or longer tail. *3* Do not weave in ends as you go. *4* A colors and B colors are randomly placed while working in Fibonacci Sequence. *5* Cuffs are worked in the round after the sleeve seam has been joined.

Body
With circular needle and any A color and using long-tail loop cast-on, cast on 127 (143, 159, 175, 191) stitches. Join any B color at tail-end of needle and purl across row (A and B are at same end of needle); turn. Work in Column Pattern following Body Fibonacci Sequence until piece measures 13 (13, 13½, 14, 14)", end with a RS A row (row 1 of pattern).

Divide for fronts and back: Next row (RS B row) Work 26 (29, 32, 35, 38) stitches and place on hold for right front, using p2tog bind-off, bind off 11 (13, 15, 17, 19) stitches for right underarm, work 53 (59, 65, 71, 77) stitches and place on hold for back, bind off 11 (13, 15, 17, 19) stitches for left underarm, work 26 (29, 32, 35, 38) stitches (left front).

Left front
Work 10 rows.
Shape V-neck
SSK at end of every other RS A row 11 (11, 12, 12, 13) times—15 (18, 20, 23, 25) stitches. Work even until piece measures approximately 22½ (23, 24, 25, 25½)", end with a RS B row. Place stitches on hold.

Back
Place 53 (59, 65, 71, 77) stitches of back on needle. With WS facing, join A and B at armhole. Work even until piece measures same length as left front. Place stitches on hold.

Right front
Place 26 (29, 32, 35, 38) stitches of right front on needle. With WS facing, join A and B at armhole. Work as for left front EXCEPT k2tog at beginning of every other RS A row for V-neck. When piece measures same length as left front, leave stitches on needle. Do not cut B.
Join shoulders
With WS together and B, work 3-needle YO bind-off to join the 15 (18, 20, 23, 25) stitches of right shoulder, continue across back of neck with YO bind-off until 15 (18, 20, 23, 25) stitches remain. Join left shoulder with 3-needle YO bind-off.

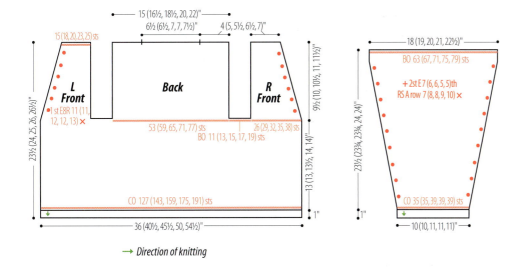

15 (16½, 18½, 20, 22)"

6½ (6½, 7, 7, 7½)"   4 (5, 5½, 6½, 7)"

15 (18, 20, 23, 25) sts

L Front

Back

R Front

9½ (10, 10½, 11, 11½)"

23½ (24, 25, 26, 26½)"

1 st E8R 11 (11, 12, 12, 13) ✕

53 (59, 65, 71, 77) sts   26 (29, 32, 35, 38) sts

BO 11 (13, 15, 17, 19) sts

13 (13, 13½, 14, 14)"

CO 127 (143, 159, 175, 191) sts

1"

36 (40½, 45½, 50, 54½)"

→ *Direction of knitting*

18 (19, 20, 21, 22½)"

BO 63 (67, 71, 75, 79) sts

+ 2st E 7 (6, 6, 5, 5)th
RS A row 7 (8, 8, 9, 10) ✕

23½ (23¾, 23¾, 24, 24)"

CO 35 (35, 39, 39, 39) sts

1"

10 (10, 11, 11, 11)"

The Fibonacci sequence brings balance and harmony to design. This mathematical sequence is named after Leonardo of Pisa, known as Fibonacci. A Fibonacci sequence with 0 as its first number is 0-1-1-2-3-5-8-13-21-34, etc. After the two initial values, each number is the sum of the two numbers immediately preceding it.

In the Cardi-Vest, the sequence determines the number of rows worked for each color. Any portion of the sequence can be used. The sleeve's 2-3-5-8 segment gives a lively, vibrant look. The body's 3-5-8-13 segment results in fewer color changes and a more tranquil appearance. For both, the sequence moves in one direction for the A colors and in the opposite direction for the B colors.

Sleeves

Working as for body, cast on 35 (35, 39, 39, 39) stitches and purl 1 row. Work in Column Pattern following Sleeve Fibonacci Sequence for 1", then work double increase in 4th stitch from beginning and end of every 7th (6th, 6th, 5th, 5th) RS A row 7 (8, 8, 9, 10) times—63 (67, 71, 75, 79) stitches. Work even until piece measures 23½ (23¾, 23¾, 24, 24)", end with WS B row. With RS facing and A, p2tog bind off.

Finishing

Join sleeve seam With RS facing, any A color, and circular needle, pick up and knit 1 stitch for every 2 Vs along one side of sleeve. Pick up and knit same number of stitches down other side of same sleeve. With WS together, work 3-needle YO bind-off. Repeat for other sleeve seam.

Note Use A colors for all bands. Select one color to pick up and knit stitches and use that same color for the first round or row. Then change to a different color after every row or round of the bands.

Wristband With RS facing and double-pointed needles, pick up and knit 33 (33, 37, 37, 37) stitches around lower sleeve edge. Join and mark beginning of round. Purl 2 rounds, knit 2 rounds, purl 3 rounds. Bind off.

Front, lower, and back neck bands With RS facing and circular needle, begin at right shoulder and pick up and knit 1 stitch in each column across back neck and 2 stitches for every 3 Vs along left front, place corner marker, 1 stitch for each column across lower edge, place corner marker, and 2 stitches for every 3 Vs along right front. Place beginning-of-round marker and join. Purl 1 round. **Increase round 1** *Purl to 1 stitch before corner marker, M1, p1, slip marker, p1, M1; repeat from *, purl to end of round. **Next round** Knit, making 7 (7, 8, 9, 9) YO buttonholes evenly spaced along left front (man's) or right front (woman's), working top buttonhole at the base of V-neck shaping and bottom buttonhole 2 stitches above marker at lower corner. **Increase round 2** *Knit to 1 stitch before corner marker, M1, k1, slip marker, k1, M1; repeat from *, knit to end of round. Purl 2 rounds. Bind off.

Armband With RS facing and smaller circular needle, begin at corner of underarm bind-off and pick up and knit 73 (77, 81, 85, 89) stitches along the sides of the armhole, turn. Knit WS row, turn. Purl RS row, slide. **Buttonhole row** (RS) K3 (2, 4, 3, 5), [yo, k2tog, k4] 11 (12, 12, 13, 13) times, yo, k2tog, k2 (1, 3, 2, 4), slide. **Row 4** (RS) Knit, slide. **Next 3 rows** Purl, slide. Bind off. Block pieces. Sew ends of armbands to underarm bind-off. Sew buttons onto front and top of sleeves to match buttonholes.

Body Fibonacci Sequence

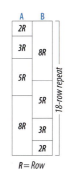

A	B
3R	
5R	13R
8R	
	8R
13R	5R
3R	

29-row repeat

R = Row

As you work Column Pattern, change A color after *13 rows, 8 rows, 5 rows, 3 rows; repeat from *. AT SAME TIME, change B after **3 rows, 5 rows, 8 rows, 13 rows; repeat from **.

Sleeve Fibonacci Sequence

A	B
2R	
3R	8R
5R	
	5R
8R	3R
	2R

18-row repeat

R = Row

As you work Column Pattern, change A color after *8 rows, 5 rows, 3 rows, 2 rows; repeat from *. AT SAME TIME, change B after **2 rows, 3 rows, 5 rows, 8 rows; repeat from **.

 BOOKS

23

Fibonacci Cardi-Vest

Removable sleeves paved the way to sample another segment of the Fibonacci sequence.

Parisienne

Joining the pieces with a 3-needle bind-off creates a beautiful braid, giving the jacket that certain Chanel touch.

Check Pattern OVER ODD NUMBER OF STITCHES
Row 1 (RS) With A, k1, *k1b, k1; repeat from *.
Row 2 (WS) With A, knit.
Row 3 (RS) With B, k1, *k1, k1b; repeat from *, end k2.
Row 4 (WS) With B, knit.
Repeat rows 1–4 for Check Pattern.

☐ K on RS
⬛ K on WS
⬇ K1b on RS

Parisienne

INTERMEDIATE

LOOSE FIT

S (M, L, 1X)
A 40 (42, 48, 52)"
B 19 (20, 22, 24)"
C 29 (30, 31, 33)"

10cm/4"
52
20
• Over Check Pattern using larger needles

1 2 **3** 4 5 6
Light weight
A & B • 700 (775, 900, 1025) yds each

3.75mm/US 5, or size to obtain gauge
Extra needle for 3-needle bind-off

3.25mm/US 3, 80–100cm (32–40") long

9 (10, 10, 10) • 16mm/(5/8")

&
Stitch markers and holders

Small: 4 skeins each GARNSTUDIO Silke-Tweed in colors 06 (A) and 10 (B)

Note

See *Techniques*, page 138 for long-tail loop cast-on, k1b, k2tog, SSK, Make 1, 3-needle bind-off, YO buttonhole, 3-needle YO bind-off, YO, and p2tog bind-off.

Back

With larger needle and B and using long-tail loop cast-on, cast on 103 (109, 121, 131) stitches. Knit 1 row. Work in Check Pattern until piece measures approximately 11 (12, 13, 14)", end with a WS B row (row 4 of pattern).
Shape armholes
Bind off 8 (8, 10, 10) stitches at beginning of next 2 rows. Decrease 1 stitch each side every RS A row 6 (6, 8, 10) times—75 (81, 85, 91) stitches. Work even until armhole measures 7 (7, 8, 9)", end after a RS A row. Place stitches on hold.

Pocket Lining MAKE 2

With larger needle and A and using long-tail loop cast-on, cast on 28 stitches. Work in stockinette stitch (knit on RS, purl on WS) for 3½", decreasing 5 stitches equally spaced across last (RS) row—23 sts. Place stitches on hold.

Left Front

With larger needle and B and using long-tail loop cast-on, cast on 49 (53, 59, 65) stitches. Knit 1 row. Work in Check Pattern until piece measures 3½", end with a WS B row.
Place pocket: Next row Work 13 (15, 18, 21) stitches, work 23 stitches and place on hold, work to end. ***Next row*** Work 13 (15, 18, 21) stitches; with WS of lining facing, work in Check Pattern across 23 stitches of pocket lining, work to end. Work until same length as back to underarm, end with a WS B row.
Shape armhole
Bind off 8 (8, 10, 10) stitches at beginning of next row. Decrease 1 stitch at armhole edge every RS A row 6 (6, 8, 10) times—35 (39, 41, 45) stitches. Work even until armhole measures 4 (4, 5, 6)", end with a RS B row.
Shape neck
Bind off 7 (8, 9, 10) stitches at beginning of next row. Decrease 1 stitch at neck edge every RS A row 5 (6, 7, 8) times—23 (25, 25, 27) stitches. Work even until armhole measures 8 (8, 9, 10)", end with a RS A row. Place stitches on hold.

Right Front

Work as for left front, reversing armhole and neck shaping. Bind off for armhole at beginning of WS row and decrease at end of RS rows. Shape neck at beginning of RS rows.

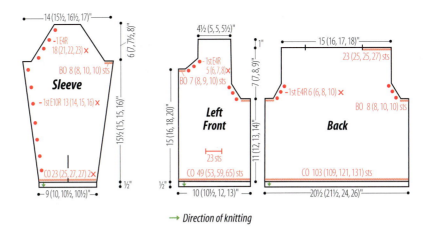

Sleeve
- 14 (15½, 16½, 17)"
- 6 (7, 7½, 8)"
- ←1 E4R
- 18 (21, 22, 23) ✕
- BO 8 (8, 10, 10) sts
- ←1st E10R 13 (14, 15, 16) ✕
- CO 23 (25, 27, 27) 2✕
- 15½ (15, 15, 16)"
- ½"
- 9 (10, 10½, 10½)"

Left Front
- 4½ (5, 5, 5½)"
- 1st E4R
- 5 (6, 7, 8) ✕
- BO 7 (8, 9, 10) sts
- 15 (16, 18, 20)"
- 1"
- 23 sts
- CO 49 (53, 59, 65) sts
- ½"
- 10 (10½, 12, 13)"

Back
- 15 (16, 17, 18)"
- 23 (25, 25, 27) sts
- ←1st E4R 6 (6, 8, 10) ✕
- BO 8 (8, 10, 10) sts
- 7 (7, 8, 9)"
- 11 (12, 13, 14)"
- CO 103 (109, 121, 131) sts
- 20½ (21½, 24, 26)"

→ *Direction of knitting*

Garter Edging

Rows 1 (RS) *& 2* (WS) With A, knit.
Rows 3 & 4 With B, knit.
Rows 5–8 Repeat rows 1–4.
Row 9 (RS) With A, knit. Turn. With A and using p2tog bind-off, bind off.

Sleeve

Cuff *With larger needle, B, and using long-tail loop cast-on, cast on 23 (25, 27, 27) stitches. Knit 1 row. Work in Check Pattern for 2½", end with a WS row. Place stitches on hold. Repeat from * for second half-cuff. Place both pieces on needle—46 (50, 54, 54) stitches.

Next row (RS) Work to last stitch of first piece, k2tog (last stitch of first piece with first stitch of second piece), work to end of row—45 (49, 53, 53) stitches. Work 1 row. Work a Make 1 increase after the first stitch and before the last stitch of the next and every following 10th row a total of 13 (14, 15, 16) times—71 (77, 83, 85) stitches. Work even until sleeve measures 15½ (15, 15, 16)", end with a WS row.
Shape cap
Bind off 8 (8, 10, 10) stitches at beginning of next 2 rows. Decrease 1 stitch at beginning and end of next row and every following 4th row a total of 18 (21, 22, 23) times—19 stitches. Place stitches on hold.

Finishing

Join shoulders With WS of back and right front together and A, work 3-needle bind-off to join 23 (25, 25, 27) stitches of right shoulders, continue across stitches of back neck with standard bind-off until 23 (25, 25, 27) stitches remain. Join left shoulders with 3-needle bind-off.

Set in sleeve With RS facing and A, pick up and knit 1 stitch for each bound-off armhole stitch and 1 stitch for every 2 rows along vertical sections of armhole. With a second needle, pick up and knit the same number of stitches along the sleeve cap. With WS together and A, join sleeve to armhole with 3-needle YO bind-off. Repeat for other sleeve.

Side and sleeve seam With RS facing and A, pick up and knit 3 stitches for every 8 rows along left sides and sleeve edges. With WS together and A, join with 3-needle YO bind-off starting at cuff. Repeat for right sides and sleeve edges, ending at cuff.

Edging

Note Work all bands with smaller needle; begin with RS facing and A.
Pocket band Work Garter Edging across pocket stitches. Sew pocket linings and ends of band in place.

Neckband Begin at right front neck and pick up and knit stitches around neck, approximately 4–5 stitches per inch. Work Garter Edging, starting with Row 2.
Button band: Row 1 With circular needle, and A, begin at left front neckband and pick up and knit 1 stitch for every 3 rows along front edge, place marker (pm), 1 corner stitch, pm, 1 stitch in each stitch across the body, pm, 1 corner stitch, pm, 1 stitch for every 3 rows along right front. *Row 2* (WS) Knit. *Row 3* (RS) With B, *knit to marker, yo, slip marker, k1, yo; repeat from * once, knit to end of row. *Row 4* Knit. *Buttonhole Row 5* (RS) With A, *knit to marker, yo, slip marker, k1, yo; repeat from * once, work 5 (6, 6, 6) evenly spaced YO buttonholes on right front, first 3" above bottom marker and last 1" below top. *Row 6* (WS) Knit. *Rows 7, 8* Repeat rows 3, 4.
Row 9 With A, *knit to marker, yo, slip marker, k1, yo; repeat from * once, knit to end of row. Bind off using p2tog bind-off.

Right cuff: Row 1 Pick up and knit 1 stitch for every 3 rows along sleeve slit, pm, 1 in corner stitch, pm, 1 in each stitch across cast-on. Continue as for Button band, working 2 YO buttonholes along slit.
Left cuff Work as for right cuff, beginning with cast-on edge and ending with slit. Sew buttons opposite buttonholes.

This is one of the few k1b patterns that can be knit using straight needles rather than circular needles. It does not involve sliding the stitches since 2 rows at a time are worked in Color A and Color B.

The hound's-tooth pattern is created by knitting one below in Rows 1 and 3 and simply knitting Rows 2 and 4. Since this creates a garter-based fabric, it lies nice and flat without curling at the edges. The fabric is stable and has a 3-D texture.

 BOOKS

Column Pattern OVER EVEN NUMBER OF STITCHES

Row 1 (RS) With A, k1, *k1, k1b; repeat from *, end k1, slide.
Row 2 (RS) With B, k1 *k1b, k1; repeat from *, end k1, turn.
Row 3 (WS) With A, p1 *p1b, p1; repeat from *, end p1, slide.
Row 4 (WS) With B, p1, *p1, p1b; repeat from *, end p1, turn.
Repeat rows 1—4 for Column Pattern.

Column Pattern

2-st repeat

☐ K on RS, p on WS
⬇ K1b on RS, p1b on WS

Yin Yang

Notes

1 See *Techniques*, page 138, for long-tail loop cast-on, k1b, p1b, slide, double increase, SSK, k2tog, k3togb, SSSKb, loop cast-on, p2tog bind-off, k2tog bind-off, YO bind-off, mattress stitch, inserting zipper, and 3-needle YO bind-off.
2 Cardigan is knit from the top down; sleeves are picked up along the armhole and worked to cuff.

1/1/1 Left Cross (1/1/1 LC)

Slip 1 stitch to cable needle, hold to front; slip 1 stitch to another cable needle, hold to back, k1; k1 from back cable needle; k1 from front cable needle: the first and third stitches cross left over right in front of the center stitch.

1/1/1 Right Cross (1/1/1 RC)

Slip 2 stitches to cable needle, hold to back, k1; slip 1 from cable needle to left needle, bring cable needle to front, k1; k1 from cable needle: the first and third stitches cross right over left in front of the center stitch.

Left Front

With A and using long-tail loop cast-on, cast on 18 (20, 22, 24) stitches. Join B at tail end of needle; purl 1 row (A and B are at same end of needle); turn. Work Column Pattern for 4 rows.
***Cable row** (RS A row)* Work 3 stitches in pattern, 1/1/1 LC, work to end of row. Continue in Column Pattern for 7 rows.
***Cable & increase row** (RS A row)* Work 3 stitches in pattern, 1/1/1 LC, work to last 2 stitches, double increase, k1—2 stitches increased. Continue in Column Pattern for 7 rows.
Repeat from * 6 times total; work even on 30 (32, 34, 36) stitches until piece measures approximately 9½ (10, 10½, 11)", end with a RS B row. Place stitches on hold.

Right Front

With A and using long-tail loop cast-on, cast on 18 (20, 22, 24) stitches. Join B at tail end of needle; purl 1 row (A and B are at same end of needle); turn. Work Column Pattern for 5 rows.
***Cable row** (RS B row)* Work to last 6 stitches, 1/1/1 RC, work to end of row. Work Column Pattern as established for 7 rows.
***Cable & increase row** (RS B row)* K1, double increase, work to last 6 stitches, 1/1/1 RC, work to end of row— 2 stitches increased. Continue in Column Pattern for 7 rows.
Repeat from * 6 times total; work even on 30 (32, 34, 36) stitches until piece measures approximately 9½ (10, 10½, 11)", end with a RS B row. Place stitches on hold.

INTERMEDIATE+

LOOSE FIT

Men's S (M, L, 1X)
A 41 (45½, 50, 54½)"
B 23 (24, 25, 26)"
C 32 (33, 34, 35)"

10cm/4"
40
14
• *over Column Pattern*

1 2 3 **4** 5 6

Medium weight
A & B • 750 (825, 925, 1025) yds each

4mm/US 6, or size to obtain gauge, 60cm (24") or longer
Extra needle for 3-needle bind-off

2 cable needles, stitch markers, stitch holders, yarn needle, sewing thread, sewing needle, 2 separating 32" zippers: 1 in each of the yarn colors

Medium: 9 balls each MISSION FALLS 1824 Wool in colors 004 Charcoal (A) and 015 Putty (B)

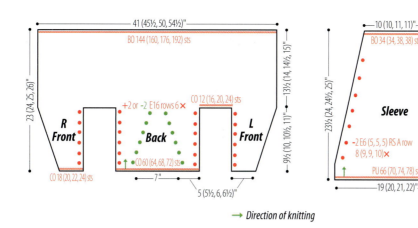

→ Direction of knitting

Back

Cast on 60 (64, 68, 72) stitches with A and purl 1 row with B as for fronts. Work Column Pattern for 4 rows.

Cable row 1 (RS A row) Work 45 (47, 49, 51) stitches in pattern, 1/1/1 LC, work 12 (14, 16, 18) stitches, slide.

Cable row 2 (RS B row) Work 12 (14, 16, 18) stitches in pattern, 1/1/1 RC, work 45 (47, 49, 51) stitches, turn. Continue in Column Pattern for 6 rows.

Cable & increase/decrease row 1 (RS A row) Work to 3 stitches before second cable, k3togb, 1/1/1 LC, work to last 2 stitches, double increase, k1, slide.

Cable & increase/decrease row 2 (RS B row) K1, double increase, work to first cable, 1/1/1 RC, SSSKb, work to end, turn. Continue in Column Pattern for 6 rows.

Repeat from * 6 times total, work even on 60 (64, 68, 72) stitches as established until piece measures approximately 9½ (10, 10½, 11)", end with a RS B row.

Join back and fronts: Next row (WS A row) Join A, work 30 (32, 34, 36) stitches of right front, loop cast on 12 (16, 20, 24) stitches for right underarm, work 60 (64, 68, 72) stitches of back, loop cast on 12 (16, 20, 24) stitches for left underarm, work 30 (32, 34, 36) stitches of left front, slide—144 (160, 176, 192) stitches.

Next row Work WS B row, purling the 12 (16, 20, 24) underarm stitches, turn.

Mark center 6 stitches of underarm. Continuing in Column Pattern with cables, establish a 1/1/1 RC before and a 1/1/1 LC after 6 marked stitches. Work until piece measures approximately 23 (24, 25, 26)", end with a non-cable RS A row, turn. With A, knit 1 row, turn. Bind off using p2tog bind off.

Join shoulders: Note Pick up and knit stitches with RS facing and A.

Pick up and knit 18 (20, 22, 24) stitches across cast-on of left front; place stitches on hold. Pick up and knit 18 (20, 22, 24) stitches across cast-on of right front. With second circular needle, pick up and knit 60 (64, 68, 72) stitches across cast-on of back. With WS together, work 3-needle YO bind-off to join right shoulders, continue YO bind-off across back neck until 18 (20, 22, 24) stitches remain. Place stitches of left front on needle; join left shoulders with 3-needle YO bind-off.

Sleeves

With RS facing and A, pick up and knit 66 (70, 74, 78) stitches along vertical sides of armhole, slide. Place marker at center of sleeve. Join B; knit 1 row (A and B are at same end of needle); turn.

Begin Column Pattern Work WS A and B rows (rows 3 and 4 of pattern).

Cable row 1 (RS A) Work to 6 stitches before marker, 1/1/1 LC, work to end of row, slide.

Cable row 2 (RS B) Work to 3 stitches after marker, 1/1/1 RC, work to end of row, turn.

The cardigan's V-neck shaping is worked along the armholes, not at the V. The Column Pattern is so flexible and forgiving that this does not distort the shape of the sweater. An added benefit: built-in shoulder shaping.

TIP Change balls of yarn behind the cables rather than at the edges. Their ends can easily be hidden behind the cable stitches. When it comes time to pick up along the front of the cardigan for the edging and to sew in the zipper, there will be no yarn ends in your way.

Continue in Column Pattern, working cables every other RS A and B rows AT SAME TIME, when sleeve measures 2½ (3, 3½, 4)" from pick up, decrease 2 stitches along each side of sleeve every 6th (5th, 5th, 5th) RS A and following B row 8 (9, 9, 10) times —34 (34, 38, 38) stitches—as follows:

Decrease row 1 (RS A row) Work to 6 stitches before end of row, k3togb, work to end, slide.

Decrease row 2 (RS B row) Work 3 stitches in pattern, SSSKb, work to end, turn.

Work even until sleeve measures approximately 23½ (24, 24½, 25)", end with a RS A row.

Begin sleeve edging: Next row With WS facing and A, SSK, knit to last 2 stitches, k2tog—32 (32, 36, 36) stitches, turn. P2tog bind off.

Finishing

Right front edging With RS facing and B and beginning at lower corner, pick up and knit one stitch for each V to shoulder seam, turn. P2tog bind off.

Left front edging With RS facing and 4-yard tail of B and beginning at shoulder seam, pick up and knit one stitch for each V to lower edge, slide. K2tog bind off.

Seams Sew straight edge at top of sleeves to underarm stitches. Sew sleeve seams using mattress stitch.

Zipper Pin zipper in place. With regular sewing thread, sew zipper in place under edging along entire length of left and right front. At the shoulder, fold the zipper tape and tack it to the back neck, overlapping the excess length of the tape.

The zipper continues to the shoulder and across the back neck, supporting the sweater's weight. Since the V-neck is shaped at the armholes, the wearer can decide how far to zip or unzip.

K1b and Cables

The man's Yin Yang Cardigan is so named because it is based on the balance of positive and negative. Although separate, the Yin and the Yang are never separated; they constitute two opposing and yet complementary aspects of one whole. The cables are symmetrically positioned, they twist in opposite directions, and their colors are reversed. The shaping along the right front armhole is light, whereas the shaping along the left front armhole is dark. The same applies to the pair of cables running down the sleeves as well as to the pair running along the sides.

The sweater is knit from the top down, allowing knitters to adjust the length as they knit. Since the yarn is quite thick, the sweater is made without side seams. The sleeves are picked up and then knit down to the cuff. The stitch orientation of the body and sleeves matches, and bulky seams are avoided.

Although many patterns start with the back of the garment, this one begins with the front yokes because they are easy. Once you have worked the front yokes, the back is simple. It takes the same increases and adds double decreases worked at the same intervals to maintain the stitch count and back width. Placing the decreases between the cables creates a triangle, which corresponds to the front V.

To keep the columns long and lean, the 'neck' increases are not placed along the V-neck but rather at the armholes. This creates stripes that run the entire length of the center front of the garment and also yields smooth cardigan edges. The column fabric is so flexible and forgiving that it can be pulled slightly on the bias with no distortion. A fringe benefit: the shoulders slant with no need for short-row shaping.

A k1b sweater with no seams and a sleek zippered opening poses a challenge: where should we hide the inevitable ends? But a k1b cable sweater provides the answer: join your yarns at the cables. The smooth fabric is not disrupted and the ends are easily hidden behind the cables.

Even the zipper follows the Yin Yang principle. I chose two 32" separating zippers in the two colors of the yarn and combined half of each. Because the V-neck shaping is positioned at the armholes, the front edge forms one continuous line and the zipper is easy to insert—straight up to the shoulder and across the back neck—allowing the wearer to decide how far to zip up. The zipper tape stabilizes the front opening and the back neck, supporting the weight of the garment. In a longer cardigan, the zipper can simply be overlapped to a lesser extent along the back neck.

Yin and Yang come back into play when it is time to finish the cardigan fronts. One edge is worked from top to bottom with the k2tog bind-off in one color, while the other edge is worked from bottom to top with the p2tog bind-off in the other color. The result is a finished edge that precisely replicates the columns of the fabric—a perfect frame for the zipper and a totally elegant finishing touch.

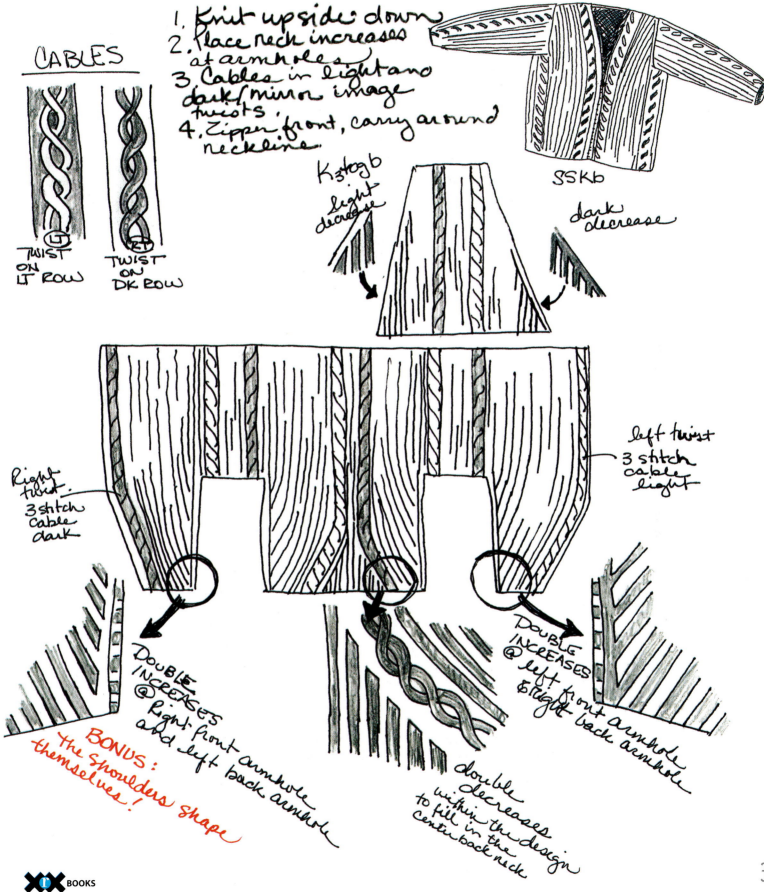

CABLES

TWIST ON LT ROW

TWIST ON DK ROW

1. Knit upside down
2. Place neck increases at armholes
3. Cables in light and dark (mirror image) twists.
4. Zipper front, carry around neckline.

K3togb
light decrease

dark decrease

SSKb

Right twist 3 stitch cable dark

left twist 3 stitch cable light

Double INCREASES @ Right front armhole and left back armhole

Double INCREASES @ left front armhole & right back armhole

double decreases within the design to fill in the center back neck

BONUS: the shoulders shape themselves!

33

East Meets West

We like this jacket so much that we made 2 versions, at 2 different gauges.

A short-repeat variegated flickers through the solid columns. For even more fun, RS and WS alternate across fronts, backs, and sleeves. Longer sleeves (about 3") double up as cuffs.

Start each piece at the same place in the color repeat so that the color stacking matches and the horizontal stripes are uniform.

Column pattern OVER ODD NUMBER OF STITCHES

Row 1 (RS) With A, k1, *k1b, k1; repeat from *, slide.
Row 2 (RS) With B, k1, *k1, k1b; repeat from *, end k2, turn.
Row 3 (WS) With A, p1, *p1b, p1; repeat from *, slide.
Row 4 (WS) With B, p1, *p1, p1b; repeat from *, end p2, turn.
Repeat rows 1–4 for Column Pattern.

Column Pattern

2-st repeat

☐ K on RS, p on WS
▓ P on RS, k on WS
↓ K1b on RS, p1b on WS
⊻ Sl 1 wyif on RS
⊻ Sl 1 wyif on WS
╱ K2tog on RS
╱ K2tog on WS

INTERMEDIATE

C
B ⎡ A ⎤
OVERSIZED FIT
S–M (L–1X, 2X–3X)
A 56 (68, 74)"
B 21 (21, 22)"
C 23 (25, 26)"

10cm/4"

32/48
10/15
• over Column Pattern using
larger needle

1 2 3 4 **5** 6
Bulky weight
A • 500 (575, 650) yds

1 2 3 **4** 5 6
Medium weight
B • 600 (700, 800) yds

1 2 **3** 4 5 6
Light weight
A • 900 (1050, 1200) yds
B • 1050 (1225, 1375) yds

4.5mm/US 7 and 5mm/US 8,
3.75mm/US 5 and 4mm/US 6 or
size to obtain gauge, 60cm (24")
or longer
Extra needle for 3-needle bind-off

2 • 25mm (1")

&
Markers, stitch holders, and
yarn needle

Large–1X: 6 balls LANG Tosca #62
Red/orange (A) and 7 balls LANG Pearl
#060 Red (B)
Small–Medium: 6 balls MANOS DEL
URUGUAY Silk Blend in color 3109
Woodland (A) and 7 balls in color 3055
Olive (B)

East meets West

Note

1 See *Techniques*, page 138, for long-tail loop cast-on, loop cast-on, k1b, p1b, k2tog, 3-needle YO bind-off, and slide. **2** The jacket pattern is given for 2 gauges. Numbers for the red jacket are first (in red) and for the green jacket second (in blue). Shared numbers are black.

Sleeves

With larger circular needle and B and using long-tail loop cast-on, cast on 41 (49, 53) 65 (75, 79) stitches. Purl 2 rows. Work Column Pattern until piece measures approximately 11", ending with RS B row (row 2 of pattern). Place stitches on hold.

Left front

With larger needle and B and using loop cast-on, cast on 42 (50, 54) 66 (76, 80) stitches. Purl 2 rows.
Work in Column Pattern with garter edging as follows:
Row 1 (RS) With A, *k1, k1b; repeat from *, end k2, slide.
Row 2 (RS) With B, k2, *k1b, k1; repeat from *, end p2, turn.
Row 3 (WS) With A, p2, *p1b, p1; repeat from *, slide.
Row 4 (WS) With B, k2, *p1, p1b; repeat from *, end p2, turn.
Repeat rows 1–4 until piece measures approximately 17 (17, 18)" from beginning, end with a RS B row. End A.
Yoke
With smaller needle and B, knit 1 row (WS). Work Yoke pattern as follows:
Row 1 (RS) Sl1 wyif, *k1, k1b; repeat from *, end k1, k2tog.
Rows 2, 4 (WS) Sl1 wyif, knit across.
Row 3 (RS) Sl1 wyif, *k1, k1b; repeat from *, end k2tog.
Repeat these 4 rows 9 (13) times more. Place remaining 22 (30, 34) 38 (48, 52) stitches on hold.

Right front

Cast on and purl 2 rows as for left front. Work in Column Pattern with garter edging as follows:
Row 1 (RS) With A, k2, *k1b, k1; repeat from *, slide.
Row 2 (RS) With B, p2, *k1, k1b; repeat from *, end k2, turn.
Row 3 (WS) With A, *p1, p1b; repeat from *, end p2, slide.
Row 4 (WS) With B, p2, *p1b, p1; repeat from *, end k2, turn.
Repeat rows 1–4 as for left front to yoke, end 1 row sooner than left front (with a RS A row). End A.

Left front, Right back panel
2-st repeat

Left front yoke
2-st repeat

Right front, Left back panel
2-st repeat

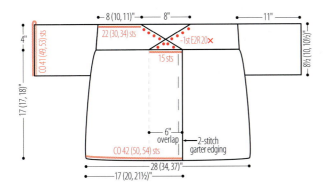

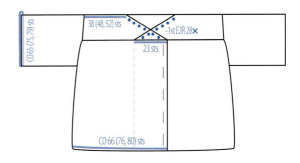

Next row, **begin buttonholes** (RS) With B, p2, k1, bind off 2 stitches, work 5 (7) stitches in pattern, bind off 2 stitches, continue in pattern to end. **Next row**, **complete buttonholes** (WS) With smaller needle and B, knit and loop cast-on 2 stitches above each bind-off—42 (50, 54) 66 (76, 80) stitches.

Yoke

Work in Yoke pattern as follows:

Row 1 (RS) Sl1 wyif, *k1b, k1; repeat from *, end k1.

Rows 2, **4** (WS) Sl1 wyif, knit to last 2 stitches, k2tog.

Row 3 (RS) Sl1 wyif, *k1, k1b; repeat from *, end k2.

Repeat last 4 rows 9 (13) more times. Place remaining 22 (30, 34) 38 (48, 52) stitches on hold.

Right front yoke

2-st repeat

Right back panel

Work as for left front to yoke. Place stitches on hold.

Left back panel

Work as for right front to yoke EXCEPT end with a RS B row. End A.

Back yoke

Note Left and Right back panels overlap at center back.

Next row, **join left and right back panels** With smaller needle, B, and WS facing, knit across left back panel. With WS of right back panel facing, place first 15 (23) stitches on hold in front of needle. (These stitches will be stitched to WS during finishing.) Continuing across row, knit remaining 27 (35, 39) 43 (53, 57) stitches of right back panel—69 (85, 93) 109 (129, 137) stitches.

Work Yoke pattern as follows:

Row 1 (RS) Sl1 wyif, *k1, k1b; repeat from *, end k2.

Row 2 (WS) Sl1 wyif, knit to last stitch, p1.

Repeat Rows 1–2 of Back Yoke pattern until piece measures same as front yoke.

Join shoulders

With WS of fronts and back together and B, work 3-needle YO bind-off to join 22 (30, 34) 38 (48, 52) stitches of right shoulder, continue across back neck with a normal bind-off (without yarn-overs) until 22 (30, 34) 38 (48, 52) stitches remain. Join left shoulder with 3-needle YO bind-off.

Assembly

Join sleeves to body Place markers along sides edges of front and back, 8½ (10, 10½)" below shoulder seam. With RS facing, smaller needle and B, and beginning at front marker, pick up and knit 20 (24, 26) 32 (37, 39) stitches to shoulder seam, 1 stitch at shoulder seam, and 20 (24, 26) 32 (37, 39) stitches to back marker—41 (49, 53) 65 (75, 79) stitches. With sleeve stitches on a second needle and WS of sleeve and body together, zig-zag bind-off as follows: *bind off 1 stitch from sleeve, bind off 1 stitch from body; repeat from * across. Join other sleeve to body.

Side/sleeve seams With RS facing and smaller needle and B, pick up and knit 1 stitch for every 2 rows (every visible stitch) along left front and left sleeve, picking up the stitches in the 'ditch' between the first and second stitches. With a second needle, pick up and knit same number of stitches along left sleeve and left back. Starting at lower edge of body, work zig-zag bind-off to cuff. Repeat for right front/back, working zig-zag bind-off from cuff to lower edge.

Stitch the 15 right back stitches to WS of yoke. Sew buttons on left front to correspond to buttonholes. Block.

Back Yoke

2-st repeat

Sweaters

40

The k1b stitch pattern breaks up the typical variegated patterning. **On the Easy Side** is made with just one hand-painted yarn; columns are formed here and there when yarn segments of the same color meet along the way.

52

Lofty mohair contrasts with compact, braided yarn for the **Block Sweater's** basket weave texture.

46

Just because **Borderline** has borders does not mean it is limited by boundaries! Pick your colors and dress up your fellow.

50

Purple trim adds zing to the autumn colors of the **Non-Repeating Sweater's** columns.

56

The Column Pattern is perfect for intarsia, with **Another Facet's** darker columns looking as if they have been superimposed on the lighter squares.

44

Bands of horizontal color form the peaks, while sparkles liven up the valleys in **Thick and Thin's** three-dimensional fabric. A touch of dazzle comes from the buttons, some decorative, some functional.

K1b Pattern OVER AN EVEN NUMBER OF STITCHES
Row 1 (RS) Slip 1 as if to purl and with yarn on WS (slip 1), *k1, k1b; repeat from *, end k1.
Row 2 (WS) Slip 1, *p1, p1b; repeat from *, end p1. Repeat rows 1–2 for K1b Pattern.

K1b Pattern
2-st repeat

☐ K on RS, p on WS
▼ K1b on RS, p1b on WS
☑ Sl 1 with yarn on WS

On the Easy Side

INTERMEDIATE

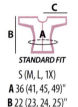

STANDARD FIT
S (M, L, 1X)
A 36 (41, 45, 49)"
B 22 (23, 24, 25)"
C 27 (28¼, 29¼, 30¼)"

10cm/4"
44
14
• over K1b Pattern

1 2 **3** 4 5 6
Light weight
1100 (1300, 1500, 1700) yds

4mm/US 6, or size to obtain gauge, 60cm (24") or longer

4mm/G

Stitch holders and yarn needle

Small: 10 skeins KOIGU Kersti in color # K 31225 (black/gray sweater)
Medium: 12 skeins KOIGU Kersti in color # K 1468 (colorful sweater)

Notes

1 See *Techniques*, page 138, for long-tail loop cast-on, loop cast-on, k1b, p1b, double increase, S2KP2, p2tog bind-off, and knit loop bind-off. *2* The sweater is knit from wrist to wrist in one piece.

First sleeve

With long-tail loop cast-on, cast on 28 (32, 36, 36) stitches. Purl 2 rows. Work K1b Pattern, increasing as follows: **Increase row** (RS) Double increase in 3rd stitch and next-to-last stitch every 3 (2½, 2¼, 1¾)" 5 (6, 7, 9) times. Work even on 48 (56, 64, 72) stitches until sleeve measures 18", end with a WS row.

Body

Working loop cast-on from edge of sleeve outward, cast on 52 stitches (for front). **Next row** (RS) K 52, work to end of row in pattern—100 (108, 116, 124) stitches. Cast on 52 stitches at other edge of sleeve (for back). **Next row** (WS) P52, work to end of row in pattern—152 (160, 168, 176) stitches.
Work all stitches in pattern until body measures 4½ (5¾, 6¾, 7¾)" from cast-on edge, end with a WS row.
Next row (RS) Work 76 (80, 84, 88) front stitches and place remaining stitches on hold. **Next row** (WS) Slip 1 (for selvedge stitch) and work to end. Slipping selvedge stitch at beginning of every WS row, work until neck opening measures 9", end with a RS row. Place stitches on hold. Place back stitches on needle. Attach yarn at neck, slip 1 (for selvedge stitch) and work in pattttern to end. Work back to match front EXCEPT slip selvedge stitch at beginning of every RS row.
Join front and back
Next row (WS) Work back stitches, then work front stitches from holder, discontinuing selvedge stitches at neck—152 (160, 168, 176) stitches. Work even until body measures 18 (20½, 22½, 24½)" from cast-on, end with a WS row.
Next row (RS) Work 52 stitches of front. Work 48 (56, 64, 72) stitches of second sleeve; with RS facing and separate length of yarn, knit loop bind off next 52 stitches of back; slide. With RS facing and another length of yarn, knit loop bind off 52 stitches of front. Turn.

Second sleeve

Continue in pattern on remaining 48 (56, 64, 72) stitches, working decrease rows to correspond to increase rows on the first sleeve as follows: **Decrease row** (RS) Slip 1, k1, S2KP2, work to last 4 stitches, S2KP2, k1—4 stitches decreased. Work even on 28 (32, 36, 36) stitches to match other sleeve, end with a WS row. Bind off with p2tog bind-off.

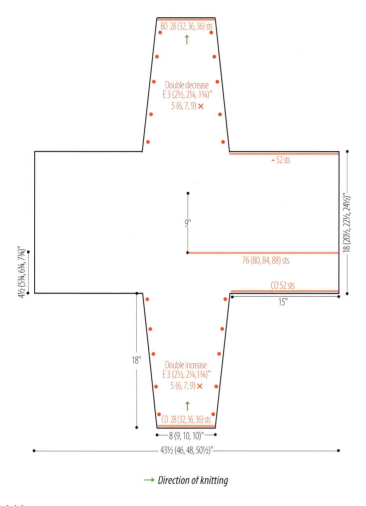

BO 28 (32, 36, 36) sts

Double decrease
E 3 (2½, 2¼, 1¾)"
5 (6, 7, 9) ✕

− 52 sts

9"

76 (80, 84, 88) sts

18 (20½, 22½, 24½)"

CO 52 sts

15"

4½ (5¾, 6¾, 7¾)"

18"

Double increase
E 3 (2½, 2¼, 1¾)"
5 (6, 7, 9) ✕

CO 28 (32, 36, 36) sts

8 (9, 10, 10)"

43½ (46, 48, 50½)"

→ *Direction of knitting*

Finishing

Block piece.

Sleeve seams With crochet hook, link selvedge stitch loops along each side of sleeve from armhole to cuff. Repeat for second sleeve.

Side seams With crochet hook, link cast-on loops of front and back from lower edge to armhole. Repeat with bound-off loops of front and back.

Fasten ends.

Linking a seam

Place pieces side by side, with RS facing you.

1 With crochet hook, catch loop at lower corner of piece.

2 Roll hook, catch loop from opposite piece and pull through loop on hook.

Repeat Step 2 until 1 loop remains on hook. Secure the last loop with an available end or an extra piece of yarn. Seam is neat and attractive on both sides. (WS, below; RS, page 39.)

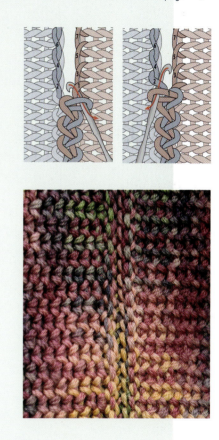

TIP To estimate the correct length of yarn for loop bind-off, loop cast on 52 stitches, leaving a tail of a few inches at each end. Cut the yarn, remove it from your knitting needle, and use that piece of yarn for the loop bind-off, adjusting your tension to use the full length of yarn. This ensures that the tension of the side seams match.

Column Pattern OVER AN ODD NUMBER OF STITCHES

Row 1 (RS) With A, k1, *k1b, k1; repeat from *, slide.

Row 2 (RS) With B, k1, *k1, k1b; repeat from *, end k2, turn.

Row 3 (WS) With A, p1, *p1b, p1; repeat from *, slide.

Row 4 (WS) With B, p1, *p1, p1b; repeat from *, end p2, turn.

Repeat rows 1–4 for Column Pattern.

Column Pattern

2-st repeat

☐ K on RS, p on WS
⤓ K1b on RS, p1b on WS

Thick and Thin

EASY +

LOOSE FIT

XS (S, M, L, 1X–2X, 3X)

A 34 (39, 44, 48, 53, 57)"

B 21 (21, 22, 23, 24, 25)"

C 28 (29, 30, 31, 32, 33)"

10cm/4"

40

14

• over Column Pattern

1 2 3 **4** 5 6

Medium weight

A • 425 (475, 525, 575, 650, 700) yds

1 2 **3** 4 5 6

Light weight

B • 425 (475, 525, 575, 650, 700) yds

4.5mm/US 7, or size to obtain
gauge, 60cm (24") long
2 extra needles for 3-needle
bind-off

14 (15, 17, 18, 21, 23) • 15mm (½")

Yarn needle and pins

Extra Small (red sweater): 5 balls
NASHUA Wooly Stripes in color WS31
Fiesta (A) and 2 balls ROWAN Kidsilk
Night in color 609 Dazzle (B)
Small (blue sweater): 6 balls Wooly
Stripes in color WS14 Blackened Jade
(A) and 3 balls Kidsilk Night in color
610 Starry Night (B)

Notes

1 See *Techniques*, page 138, for long-tail loop cast-on, k1b, p1b, slide, k2tog, p2tog bind-off, YO, kf&b, YO bind-off, and 3-needle YO bind-off. *2* Red sweater is drop-shoulder with body worked from top down, sleeves are picked up, worked down and shaped with decreases instead of increases.

Back

With A and using long-tail loop cast-on, cast on 61 (69, 77, 85, 93, 101) stitches. Join B at tail-end of needle and purl across (A and B are at same end of needle). Work in Column Pattern until piece measures approximately 11½ (11½, 12, 12½, 13, 13½)", end with a RS A row (row 1 of pattern).

Shape armholes

YO bind off 6 (6, 8, 10, 12, 14) stitches at beginning of next 2 B rows—49 (57, 61, 65, 69, 73) stitches. Work even until armholes measure 8½ (8½, 9, 9½, 10, 10½)" end with a RS B row. End A.

Buttonhole band With double strand of B, knit 2 rows. **Next row, buttonhole row** (WS) K4, *yo, k2tog, k2; repeat from * to last stitch, k1. Knit 1 row. Using p2tog bind-off, bind off all stitches.

Lower band With RS facing and double strand of B, pick up and knit 1 stitch for each column along cast-on edge. Knit 4 rows. Using p2tog bind-off, bind off all stitches.

Front

Work as for back, EXCEPT omit buttonholes on upper band (button band).

Sleeves

With A and using long-tail loop cast-on, cast on 29 (29, 31, 33, 35, 37) stitches. Join B at tail-end of needle and purl across (A and B are at same end of needle). Work in Column Pattern, AT SAME TIME on RS B row, kf&b in first and last stitch every 8th row 5 (5, 9, 13, 17, 21) times, then every 12th row 12 (12, 9, 6, 3, 0) times—63 (63, 67, 71, 75, 79) stitches. Work even until piece measures 18¾ (18¾, 18½, 18¼, 18¼, 18)". Place markers for armhole placement. Continue even for 1¾ (1¾, 2½ , 3, 3½, 4¼)", end with a WS B row. Place stitches on hold.

Lower band With RS facing and double strand of B, pick up and knit 1 stitch for each column along cast-on edge. Knit 2 rows. Using p2tog bind-off, bind off all stitches.
Repeat for second sleeve.

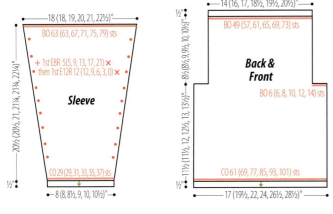

Sleeve

18 (18, 19, 20, 21, 22½)"

BO 63 (63, 67, 71, 75, 79) sts

+ 1st E8R 5(5, 9, 13, 17, 21) ✕
then 1st E12R 12 (12, 9, 6, 3, 0) ✕

20½ (20½, 21, 21¼, 21¾, 22¾)"

CO 29 (29, 31, 33, 35, 37) sts

½"

8 (8, 8½, 9, 10, 10½)"

Back & Front

½"

14 (16, 17, 18½, 19½, 20½)"

BO 49 (57, 61, 65, 69, 73) sts

8½ (8½, 9, 9½, 10, 10½)"

BO 6 (6, 8, 10, 12, 14) sts

11½ (11½, 12, 12½, 13, 13½)"

CO 61 (69, 77, 85, 93, 101) sts

½"

17 (19½, 22, 24, 26½, 28½)"

→ *Direction of knitting*

Finishing

Block pieces.

Lap buttonhole band of back over button band of front at shoulder; pin in place.

Join sleeves to body With RS facing and B, pick up and knit 63 (63, 67, 71, 75, 79) stitches evenly along front and back armhole. Place sleeve stitches on a second needle. With WS together, sleeve facing, and using double strand of B, work 3-needle YO bind-off to join.

Beginning at the markers, sew the top of sleeve to bound-off underarm stitches.

Join side and sleeve seams With RS facing and B, pick up and knit 2 stitches for every 3 Vs along sleeve and side of front. Repeat with a second needle along other edge of sleeve and side of back. Work 3-needle YO bind-off to join. Repeat for second sleeve. Sew buttons opposite buttonholes on shoulders and across front.

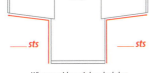

— *sts*   — *sts*

When you pick up stitches, check that the number of stitches picked up for one sleeve/side seam matches the other sleeve/side seam.

Left Column Pattern combining a thick yarn and a sock yarn. *Right* The 3-needle YO bind-off in Color B creates a seam that fits perfectly between the Color A columns. Since they stretch, the bind-offs are decorative yet functional.

Column Pattern OVER AN ODD NUMBER OF STITCHES
Row 1 (RS) With A, k1, *k1, k1b; repeat from *, end k2, slide.
Row 2 (RS) With B, k1, *k1b, k1; repeat from *, turn.
Row 3 (WS) With A, p1, *p1, p1b; repeat from *, end p2, slide.
Row 4 (WS) With B, p1, *p1b, p1; repeat from *, turn.
Repeat rows 1–4 for Column Pattern.

Column Pattern

2-st repeat

☐ *K on RS, p on WS*
☑ *K1b on RS, p1 on WS*

Borderline

EASY+

LOOSE FIT

Men's S (M, L, 1X, 2X)

A 41 (44½, 48, 51½, 54½)"
B 24 (25, 26, 26, 26)"
C 32 (33, 34, 35, 35½)"

10cm/4"
28
9.5
• over Column Pattern

1 2 3 4 **5** 6

Bulky weight
A • 385 (425, 475, 525, 550) yds
B1–B6 • 70 (75, 80, 85, 90) yds each
B7 • 0 (0, 0, 85, 90) yds

6mm/US 10, or size to obtain
gauge, 60cm (24") or longer
Extra needle for 3-needle bind-off

Five • 6mm/US 10

&

Stitch holders and stitch markers

Medium: 4 balls REYNOLDS Lopi in
color #0709 Midnight Blue (A); 1 ball
each #0047 Happy Red (B1), #0163
Quiet Purple (B2), #0484 Forest Green
(B3), #0053 Acorn (B4), #0421 Celery
(B5), #9987 Loden (B6)
For sizes 1X and 2X: #9967 Teal (B7)

Notes

1 See *Techniques*, page 138, for long-tail loop cast-on, k1b, p1b, k2tog, SSK, double increase, 3-needle bind-off, overhand knot, and slide. *2* Garter-stitch borders are worked circularly after the pieces are seamed. *3* Always change yarns at the edges and leave at least a 3" tail. Do not weave in ends as this yarn is quite thick. Since Lopi ends tend to felt together, it is sufficient to tie the ends with an overhand knot and trim to a 1" tail. Weave in ends near the edges so they do not show.

BACK

With circular needle and A and using long-tail loop cast-on, cast on 49 (53, 57, 61, 65) stitches. Join B1 at tail end of needle and purl across row (A and B1 are now at same end of needle); turn. Work Column Pattern following Color Sequence until piece measures 13½ (13½, 13¾, 12¾, 12)" from beginning. Place marker for armhole. Continue until piece measures approximately 22¾ (23¾, 24¾, 24¾, 24¾)" from beginning, end with a RS A row (row 1 of pattern). Place stitches on hold.

FRONT

Work as for back until piece measures approximately 19¾ (20¾, 21¾, 21¾, 21¾)", end with a WS B row.
Shape left front neck

Next row (RS A row) Work 18 (20, 21, 23, 24) stitches in pattern, place next 13 (13, 15, 15, 17) stitches on hold for neck, place last 18 (20, 21, 23, 24) stitches on hold for right neck and shoulder, slide.

Next 2 RS B rows Work to 2 stitches before neck, SSK, turn—16, (18, 19, 21, 22) stitches. Work even until left front measures same length as back, end with a RS A row. Place stitches on hold.
Shape right front neck

Place 18 (20, 21, 23, 24) stitches on needle. With RS facing, attach A and B at neck edge. Work as for left front, EXCEPT work decrease rows as follows: k2tog, work to end, turn. When same length as back, leave stitches on needle. Do not cut A.
Join shoulders

With WS together, circular needle, and A, work 3-needle bind-off to join 16 (18, 19, 21, 22) stitches of right shoulder, continue to bind off across back neck until 16 (18, 19, 21, 22) stitches remain. Join left shoulder with 3-needle bind-off.

Color sequence

*Change B color after 3 B rows of Column Pattern as follows: B1, B2, B3, B4, B5, B6, and for sizes 1X and 2X only, B7; repeat from *.

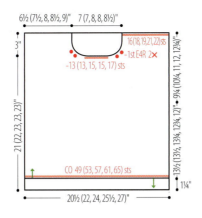

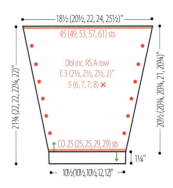

→ Direction of knitting

SLEEVES

With circular needle and A and using long-tail loop cast-on, cast on 25 (25, 25, 29, 29) stitches. Join B1 at tail end of needle and purl across row (A & B1 are now at same end of needle); turn. Work Column Pattern following Color Sequence, AT SAME TIME, approximately every 3 (2½, 2½, 2½, 2)", work double increase in 3rd stitch from beginning and end of RS A row a total of 5 (6, 7, 7, 8) times—45 (49, 53, 57, 61) stitches. Work even until piece measures 20½ (20¾, 20¾, 21, 20¾)". Place stitches on hold.

FINISHING

Block pieces.

Join sleeves and body With RS facing, circular needle, and A, pick up and knit 45 (49, 53, 57, 61) stitches between armhole markers along one side of front and back. Place sleeve stitches on other circular needle. With WS together, body facing, and A, work 3-needle bind-off. Repeat for other sleeve and other side of body.

Join sleeve and side seams With RS facing and A, pick up and knit 1 stitch for every V along one sleeve and side of front. With a second needle and second ball of A, pick up and knit the same number of stitches along other edge of that sleeve and side of back. With WS together, front facing, and A, work 3-needle bind off. Repeat for other sleeve and side seam.

Bottom band With RS facing, circular needle and A, pick up and knit 1 stitch for each column around bottom of sweater—approximately 96 (104, 112, 120, 128) stitches. Join. [Purl 1 round, knit 1 round] 3 times. Purl 1 round. With B3, knit 1 round. Bind off in purl.

Sleeve band Work as for bottom band, EXCEPT use double-pointed needles, pick up and knit 24 (24, 24, 28, 28) stitches along cast-on edge of sleeve, and use B1 to knit last round and to bind off.

Neckband Work as for bottom band, EXCEPT use double-pointed needles, begin at left shoulder, pick up and knit 10 stitches down left neck, knit 13 (13, 15, 15, 17) front stitches from hold, pick up and knit 10 stitches up right neck, pick up and knit 17 (17, 19, 19, 21) across back neck—50 (50, 54, 54, 58) stitches, and use B2 to knit last round and to bind off.

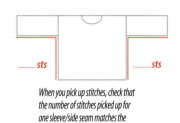

sts   sts

When you pick up stitches, check that the number of stitches picked up for one sleeve/side seam matches the other sleeve/side seam.

The name comes from the garter-stitch borders that are worked circularly after the individual pieces have been assembled. These borders are seamless and, since they are worked after the fact, they all look the same—each one finishing with different contrast colors to create the 'Borderline.'

Borderline

Seamless garter bands are worked after the fact and bordered with lines of contrasting colors.

Non-Repeating Sweater

Non-Repeating because the color pattern would only repeat after 240 rows, far beyond the length of a sweater. The three 'greens' and five 'browns' are juxtaposed in different arrangements throughout, influencing the adjacent shades to create astounding color depth and variation.

Column Pattern OVER AN ODD NUMBER OF STITCHES
Row 1 (RS) With A, k1, *k1, k1b; repeat from *, end k2, slide.
Row 2 (RS) With B, k1, *k1b, k1; repeat from *, turn.
Row 3 (WS) With A, p1, *p1, p1b; repeat from *, end p2, slide.
Row 4 (WS) With B, p1, *p1b, p1; repeat from *, turn.
Repeat rows 1–4 for Column Pattern.

Column Pattern

2-st repeat

☐ K on RS, p on RS
☑ K1b on RS, p1B on WS

Non-Repeating Sweater

INTERMEDIATE

STANDARD FIT

S-M (L, 1X, 2X, 3X)
A 39 (44, 48, 53, 57)"
B 21½ (22½, 23½, 24½, 25¾)"
C 29 (30, 31, 32, 33)"

10cm/4"

40
14
• over Column Pattern

1 2 3 **4** 5 6

Medium weight
A1–A3 • 220 (250, 275, 300, 350) yds each
B1–B5 • 135 (155, 170, 190, 210) yds each
A4 • 90 (100, 115, 125, 140) yds

4.5mm/US 7, or size to obtain gauge, 40cm (16") and 60cm (24") or longer
Extra needle for 3-needle bind-off

&

Stitch markers and holders

Small–Medium: 1 ball each NASHUA HANDKNITS Creative Focus Worsted in 3112 Evergreen (A1), 1450 Blue Pine (A2), 4899 Khaki (A3), 1715 Delphinium (A4) 0410 Espresso (B1), 2025 Syrah (B2), 3729 Rust (B3), 2124 Cordovan (B4) 2190 Copper (B5)

Notes

1 See *Techniques*, page 138, for long-tail loop cast-on, k1b, p1b, slide, kf&b, k2tog, SSK, overhand knot, YO bind-off, 3-needle YO bind-off, loop bind-off, and garter-stitch graft. *2* Do not weave in ends: tie in overhand knots and leave as fringe along the seams. Only weave in ends near garment edges so they do not show.

Back

With longer circular needle and A1 and using long-tail loop cast-on, cast on 69 (77, 85, 93, 101) stitches. Join B1 at tail-end of needle and purl across row (A1 and B1 are at the same end of needle); turn. Work Column Pattern following Color Sequences until piece measures 12 (12½, 13, 13½, 14)" from beginning, end with a RS A row (row 1 of pattern).
Shape armholes
Using YO bind-off, bind off 7 (8, 9, 11, 13) stitches at beginning of next 2 B rows—55 (61, 67, 71, 75) stitches. Work even in pattern until armhole measures approximately 9 (9½, 10, 10½, 11¼)", end with a WS B row.
Next row (RS) With A4, work in pattern. Place stitches on hold.

Front

Work as for back until armholes measure approximately 6 (6½, 7, 7½, 8¼)", end with a WS B row.
Shape left front neck
Next row (RS A row) Work 21 (24, 26, 28, 29) stitches in pattern, place next 13 (13, 15, 15, 17) stitches on hold for neck, place last 21 (24, 26, 28, 29) stitches on hold for right neck and shoulder, slide. **Next 5 RS B rows** Work to 2 stitches before neck, SSK, turn—16 (19, 21, 23, 24) stitches. Work even until left front measures same length as back, end with a WS B row. **Next row** (RS) With A4, work in pattern. Place stitches on hold.
Shape right front neck
Place 21 (24, 26, 28, 29) stitches on needle. With RS facing, attach A and B at neck edge. Work as for left front EXCEPT work decrease rows as follows: k2tog, work to end, turn. When same length as back, leave stitches on needle. Do not cut A4.
Join shoulders With WS together and A4, work 3-needle YO bind-off to join 16 (19, 21, 23, 24) stitches of right shoulder, continue to YO bind off across back of neck until 16 (19, 21, 23, 24) stitches remain. Join left shoulder with 3-needle YO bind-off.

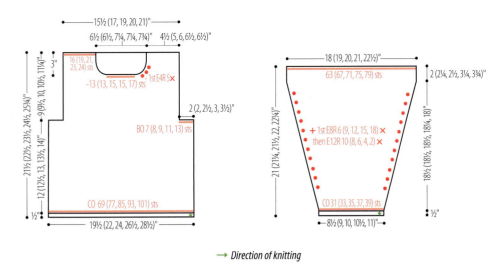

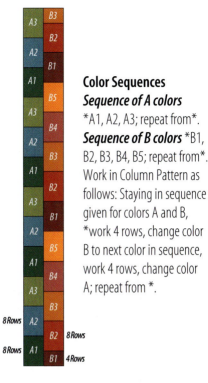

→ Direction of knitting

Color Sequences

Sequence of A colors
A1, A2, A3; repeat from.

Sequence of B colors
B1, B2, B3, B4, B5; repeat from. Work in Column Pattern as follows: Staying in sequence given for colors A and B, *work 4 rows, change color B to next color in sequence, work 4 rows, change color A; repeat from *.

Sleeves

With longer circular needle, A1, and using long-tail loop cast-on, cast on 31 (33, 35, 37, 39) stitches. Join B1 at tail-end of needle and purl across row (A1 and B1 are at same end of needle); turn. Work Column Pattern following Color Sequences, AT SAME TIME, kf&b in first and last stitch of every 8th RS B row 6 (9, 12, 15, 18) times, then every 12th RS B row 10 (8, 6, 4, 2) times—63 (67, 71, 75, 79) stitches. Work even until piece measures 18½ (18½, 18½, 18¼, 18)"; place markers at each end of row for armhole placement. Continue even for 2 (2¼, 2½, 3¼, 3¾)", end with WS B row. **Next row** (RS) With A4, work in pattern. Place stitches on hold.

Lower sleeve border With RS facing and A4, pick up and knit 1 stitch for each column across bottom of sleeve—31 (33, 35, 37, 39) stitches. Knit 1 row.

Begin Garter Border With loop cast-on, cast 3 stitches onto left needle. **Row 1** (RS) P2, p2tog (border stitch together with a sleeve stitch). **Row 2** (WS) P3. Repeat Rows 1–2 across sleeve. Bind off last 3 stitches. Repeat for other sleeve.

Finishing

Block pieces.

Note For all joins, bands, and borders, pick up and knit with RS facing and A4.

Join sleeves and body With longer circular needle, pick up and knit 7 (8, 9, 11, 13) stitches along left front underarm bind-off, 63 (67, 71, 75, 79) stitches along front and back armhole, and 7 (8, 9, 11, 13) stitches along back underarm bind-off—77 (83, 89, 97, 105) stitches. With RS facing, second circular needle, and A4, pick up and knit 7 (8, 9, 11, 13) stitches along side of sleeve between marker and bind-off, work in pattern across sleeve stitches, and pick up and knit 7 (8, 9, 11, 13) stitches along other side of sleeve above marker. Do not cut yarn. With WS together, body facing, and A4, work 3-needle YO bind-off. Join right sleeve to body in same way.

Neckband With 16" circular needle and beginning at shoulder, pick up and knit approximately 72 (72, 74, 74, 76) stitches evenly around neck edge. Place marker and join. Purl 1 round. Work Garter Border as for sleeve.

Lower border for front and back Pick up and knit 69 (77, 85, 93, 101) stitches across bottom of front and work Garter Border as for sleeve. Repeat for back.

Join sleeve and side seams With circular needle, pick up and knit 2 stitches for every 3 Vs along one sleeve and side of front. With a second needle and other end of A4, pick up and knit the same number of stitches along other side of that sleeve and side of back. With WS together, front of body facing, and A4, work 3-needle YO bind-off. Join other sleeve and side seam.

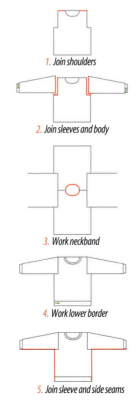

1. Join shoulders

2. Join sleeves and body

3. Work neckband

4. Work lower border

5. Join sleeve and side seams

INTERMEDIATE

STANDARD FIT

S (M, L, 1X, 2X–3X)
A 35 (40, 45, 50, 55)"
B 21 (22, 23, 24¼, 25½)"
C 29 (30, 31, 32, 33)"

10cm/4"

40

13

• over 2×2 Block Pattern

1 2 3 **4** 5 6

Medium weight
A • 550 (625, 700, 800, 875) yds
B • 675 (775, 850, 975, 1075) yds

4mm/US 6, or size to obtain
gauge, 40cm (16") and 60cm
(24") or longer

&

Stitch holders, stitch markers, and
yarn needle

Small: 5 skeins FIESTA WaterMark in
color 15117 Iris and 4 skeins Socorro in
color 27117 Iris

The Block Sweater

Notes

1 See *Techniques*, page 138, for double loop cast-on, kf&b, k1b, p1b, S2KP2, p2tog, butterfly, YO bind-off, 3-needle YO bind-off, and slide. *2* Do not change yarns in the middle of a row. *3* Split strands of textured yarn (Socorro) for sewing.

Back

With longer needle, 2 strands of Socorro held together and using double loop cast-on, cast on 58 (66, 74, 82, 90) stitches, turn. Continuing with 1 strand of Socorro, purl 2 rows. Join Watermark, work 2×2 Block Pattern until piece measures approximately 12 (12½, 13, 13½, 14)", end with row 1, 5, 9, or 13 of pattern.
Shape armholes
Bind off 4 (6, 8, 10, 12) stitches at beginning of next 2 rows—50 (54, 58, 62, 66) stitches. Work even until armhole measures approximately 8½ (9, 9½, 10, 10½)", end with Row 8 or 16. Place stitches on hold.

Front

Work as for back until armholes measure approximately 5½ (6, 6¾, 7½, 8¼)", end with row 5 or 13 of pattern.
Shape neck
Next row (RS) Work 14 (16, 18, 20, 22) stitches and place on hold for left front, work 22 stitches and place on hold for neck, work 14 (16, 18, 20, 22) stitches (right front).
Right front Work even until armhole measures 9½ (10, 10¾, 11½, 12¼)", end with row 8 or 16. Place stitches on hold.
Left front Place 14 (16, 18, 20, 22) stitches of left front on needle. With WS facing, join yarns and work even until same length as right front. Leave stitches on needle. Do not cut Socorro.
Join shoulders
With RS together and Socorro, work 3-needle YO bind-off to join 14 (16, 18, 20, 22) stitches of left shoulder, continue across back neck with YO bind-off until 14 (16, 18, 20, 22) stitches remain. Join right shoulder with 3-needle YO bind-off.

Sleeves

Working as for back, cast on 30 (34, 34, 38, 38) stitches and purl 2 rows. Work increases as follows: Kf&b, work to last stitch, kf&b on RS rows every 8th row 0 (0, 0, 0, 6) times, every 12th row 8 (8, 16, 16, 12) times, every 16th row 6 (6, 0, 0, 0) times—58 (62, 66, 70, 74) stitches. Work even until piece measures 21 (21½, 22, 22½, 23)". Bind off with YO bind-off.

2×2 Block Pattern MULTIPLE OF 4 + 2

Note For rows 1–8, A is WaterMark and B is Socorro

Row 1 (RS) With A, k1, *k1b, k2, k1b; repeat from *, k1, slide.

Row 2 (RS) With B, k1, *k1, (k1b) 2 times, k1; repeat from *, k1, turn.

Row 3 (WS) With A, p1, *p1b, p2, p1b; repeat from *, p1, slide.

Row 4 (WS) With B, p1, *p1, (p1b) 2 times, p1; repeat from *, p1, turn.

Rows 5–8 Repeat rows 1–4.

Rows 9–16 Repeat rows 1–8 EXCEPT A is Socorro and B is WaterMark.

Repeat rows 1–16 for 2×2 Block Pattern.

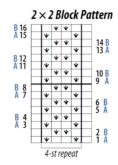

2 × 2 Block Pattern

☐ K on RS, p on WS

↓ K1b on RS, p1b on WS

Chart note
Rows 1–8 A is WaterMark, B is Socorro
Rows 9–16 A is Socorro, B is WaterMark

4-st repeat

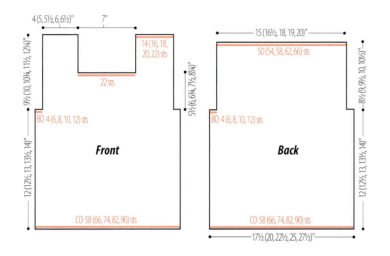

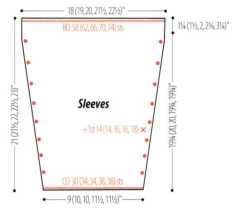

Finishing

Join sleeve and side seams Set in sleeves, centering sleeve caps approximately 1" in front of shoulder seam. Sew sleeve and side seams.

Neckband

With RS facing, shorter needle and Socorro and marking corner stitches, begin at right shoulder and pick up and knit 22 stitches of back neck, 1 corner stitch, 2 stitches for every 3 Vs along left neck edge, 1 corner stitch, 22 stitches of front neck, 1 corner stitch, 2 stitches for every 3 Vs along right neck edge, 1 corner stitch. Join. ***Round 1*** *Purl to corner stitch, k1; repeat from * around. ***Round 2*** *Knit to 1 stitch before corner stitch, S2KP2; repeat from * 3 times, knit to last 2 stitches, S2KP2 with first stitch of round. Repeat last 2 rounds 3 more times; work round 1.

Edging

With RS facing and loop cast-on, cast 2 stitches onto left needle. ***Row 1*** (RS) P1, p2tog (edging stitch together with neckband stitch), turn. ***Row 2*** (WS) P2, turn. Repeat rows 1–2 until 2 stitches remain. Graft to cast-on stitches.

TIP The following is an optional step that will facilitate assembly later on. Make a butterfly with several yards of yarn as the tail for the cast-on (page 142). By having this tail prepared, there is no need to attach a new piece of yarn when it is time for sewing the seams. Pin the butterfly to the work so it doesn't get in the way.

Longer floats extending behind 2 stitches give the 2×2 Block Pattern a looser gauge than the 1×1 Column Pattern, so it is worked on relatively small needles.

Block Sweater

The square neckline with small block edging mirrors the larger overall block pattern.

Another Facet

What knitting book would be complete without a tribute to Kaffe Fassett's sense of color and geometrical design?

54

Column Pattern OVER EVEN NUMBER OF STITCHES

Row 1 (RS) With A, k1, *k1, k1b; repeat from * end k1, slide.
Row 2 (RS) With B, k1, *k1b, k1; repeat from * end k1, turn.
Row 3 (WS) With A, p1, *p1b, p1; repeat from * end p1, slide.
Row 4 (WS) With B, p1, *p1, p1b; repeat from * end p1, turn.

Column Pattern

2-st repeat

☐ K on RS, p on RS
✔ K1b on RS, p1B on WS

EXPERIENCED

LOOSE FIT

Men's S–M (L–1X)
A 45 (53)"
B 24 (25)"
C 30¼ (33¾)"

10cm/4"

52 16

• over Column Pattern
*Each 8-stitch, 24-row block
measures 2" x 1⅞"*

1 2 **3** 4 5 6

Light weight
A1–A6, A9 • 110 (130) yds each
A7, A8, A10 • 50 (75) yds each
B1, B6 • 250 (300) yds each
B2–B5 • 150 (175) yds each

3.5mm/US 4, or size to obtain
gauge 40cm (16") and 60cm (24")
or longer
Extra needle for 3-needle bind-off

3.5mm/US 4

&

Stitch markers, stitch holders, and
yarn needle

Small–Medium: 1 ball each ROWAN
Felted Tweed 141 Maritime (A1), 142
Melody (A2), 146 Herb (A3), 147 Dragon
(A4), 152 Watery (A5), 148 Angel Delight
(A6), 155 Avocado (A7), 157 Camel
(A8), 143 Gilt (A9), 154 Ginger (A10),
145 Treacle (B2), 151 Bilberry (B3), 153
Phantom (B4), 158 Pine (B5), 159 Carbon
(B6), and 2 balls 133 Midnight (B1)

Another Facet

Notes

1 See *Techniques*, page 138, for loop cast-on, long-tail loop cast-on, k1b, p1b, Make 1, SSK, k2tog, YO bind-off, 3-needle YO bind-off, grafting, intarsia, and slide. *2* At color change on intarsia rows, pick up new A color from under the old A color. *3* The color blocks are small enough to simply use lengths of yarn without winding them onto bobbins. *4* Neck is bordered with a 4-stitch garter band, bottom of body and sleeves with a 6-stitch garter band.

Back

With B1, circular needle, and using long-tail loop cast-on, cast on 90 (106) stitches. Purl 1 row.
Work in Column Pattern following Color Chart: Intarsia Row 1 (RS) With A, k1, *[k1, k1b] 4 times, place marker (pm); repeat from *, changing A color every 8 stitches; k1, slide. ***Row 2*** (RS) With B1, k1, *k1b, k1; repeat from *, end k1, turn. ***Intarsia Row 3*** (WS) With A, p1, *[p1b, p1] to marker, slip marker (sm); repeat from *, changing A color at marker; p1, slide., ***Row 4*** (WS) With B1, p1, *p1, p1b; repeat from *, end p1, turn. Repeat Rows 1–4 a total of 3 times—12 rows. End B1, add B6. After 12 more rows, change A colors. Continue, following Color Chart, changing A and B colors as indicated, until piece is 8 A blocks high, end with a RS A row, slide.
Shape armholes
Next row Bind off 8 stitches at beginning of next 2 B rows—74 (90) stitches. Work even until armholes measure 9 (10)", end with a WS B row. Place stitches on hold.

Front

Work as for back until armholes measure 6 (7)", ending with a WS B row.
Shape left front neck
Next row (RS A row) Work 31 (38) stitches, leave remaining stitches on hold for right front, slide.
Decrease next 8 (9) RS B rows Work to last 2 sts, SSK—23 (29) stitches.
Work even until armhole measures same length as back to shoulder, ending with a WS B row. Place stitches on hold.
Shape right front neck
Place remaining 43 (52) stitches from holder on needle.
Next row (RS A row) Join A, YO bind-off 12 (14) stitches, work to end of row, slide. Join B at neck edge.
Work as for left front neck EXCEPT work k2tog decreases at beginning of RS B rows.
Join shoulders With WS together and B, work 3-needle YO bind-off to join the 23 (29) stitches of the right shoulder, continue across back of neck with YO bind-off until 23 (29) stitches remain. Join left shoulder with 3-needle YO bind-off.

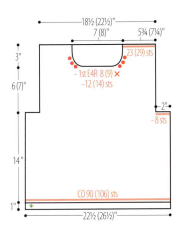

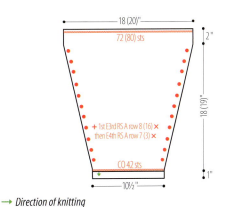

18½ (22½)"
7 (8)" 5¾ (7¼)"
23 (29) sts
– 1st E4R 8 (9) ✕
–12 (14) sts
3"
6 (7)"
– 2"
– 8 sts
14"
CO 90 (106) sts
1"
22½ (26½)"

18 (20)"
72 (80) sts
2"
+ 1st E3rd RS A row 8 (16) ✕
then E4th RS A row 7 (3) ✕
18 (19)"
CO 42 sts
1"
10½"

→ Direction of knitting

Simplified back neck shaping is the result when you dip in a curve along the back while picking up stitches for the neckband. The extra fabric lies neatly against the inside of the neckband, a technique that can give shape to any vest or sweater.

Sleeves

Cast on 42 stitches. Purl 1 row. Work Column Pattern, following Color Chart, AT SAME TIME after 1", increase 1 stitch after first stitch and before last stitch every 3rd RS A row 8 (16) times, then every 4th RS A row 7 (3) times—72 (80) stitches.

Work even until sleeve measures 18 (19)", or 2" less than desired length. Work even for approximately 2", end with a completed block of color and a WS B row. Bind off with YO bind-off.

Sew sleeve bind-off to vertical edge of armholes. Sew 2" at top of sleeves to bound-off armhole stitches. Sew side and sleeve seams.

Neckband With RS facing and B1, pick up and knit approximately 52 (60) stitches along front neck edge, 28 (32) along back neck edge, picking up one stitch per column, dipping into the fabric as follows: pick up 5 stitches along the row at the edge of the fabric, then pick up 5 stitches one row from the edge, then 8 (12) stitches 2 rows from the edge; pick up 5 stitches 1 row from the edge of the fabric, then pick up 5 stitches at the edge—80 (92) stitches. Join. Purl 1 round.

Chart note
The B color is worked across all stitches of the row, changing after 12 rows once, then every 24 rows; A colors change every 8 stitches across each row.

With loop cast-on, cast on 4 stitches and begin garter ridge edge: ***Row 1*** (RS) With B1, p3, p2tog. ***Row 2*** With B2, p4. ***Row 3*** With B2, p3, p2tog. ***Row 4*** With B1, p4. Repeat rows 1–4 around neck opening. Graft last 4 stitches to the cast-on stitches.

Lower band With RS facing, B1, and longer needle, pick up and knit 176 (208) stitches around bottom of sweater (1 stitch in each column). Purl 1 round. With loop cast-on, cast on 6 stitches and begin garter ridge edge: ***Row 1*** (RS) With B1, p5, p2tog, turn. ***Row 2*** With B2, p6. ***Row 3*** With B2, p5, p2tog. ***Row 4*** With B1, p6. Repeat rows 1–4 around sweater. Graft last 6 stitches to the cast-on stitches.

Sleeve band Work as for lower body band EXCEPT use dpns and pick up 40 (44) stitches along bottom of sleeve.

Weave in ends. Block pieces.

Color Chart, A colors

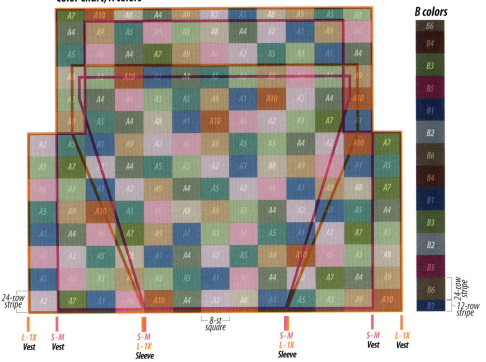

B colors

B6
B4
B3
B5
B1
B2
B6
B4
B1
B3
B2
B5
B6
B1
24-row stripe
12-row stripe

24-row stripe
8-st square

L-1X Vest S-M Vest S-M / L-1X Sleeve L-1X / S-M Sleeve S-M Vest L-1X Vest

Wardrobe Building

72

Made of sumptuous and sublime silk yarn, the sleek texture and rich colors of the **Chevron Camisole** blend in perfect harmony with each other.

70

With its offset shaping and offset band of color, the asymmetrical **Offset Tabard** can be worn in different ways, giving you stylish options.

66

The delicate **T-V Top** would be T-shaped if it were not for the V-shaped insert.

60

European linen and European styling make the
Belle Flare Duo a real asset to any wardrobe.
With its myriad of stitch patterns, it will hold your
interest throughout.

74

Slip a needle-case or lipstick into this beautiful
Beaded Necklace.

Belle Flare Duo

Notes

1 See *Techniques*, page 138 for long-tail loop cast-on, k1b, p1b, p2tog, k2tog, loop cast-on, 4-strand braid, Make 1, YO, slip 1 with yarn in front or back (sl1 wyif, sl1 wyib), YO bind-off, and crab stitch crochet. *2* Change colors loosely at the beginning of the rounds in the skirt. *3* Start new skeins at beginning of round in skirt, using weaver's knot. *4* To adjust length of skirt, adjust the length of sections 2–7. Changing the length of each section by ¼" changes the skirt length by 1½". *5* Skirt is worked from waist down, and top is worked from shoulders down.

Skirt

Note for skirt Color A is solid, B is variegated

Section 1 Upper border with eyelets for drawstring

With A and long-tail loop cast on, cast-on 200 (224, 248, 272, 296) stitches, turn. Knit 1 row (WS). Purl 1 row. Do not turn. Join and mark beginning of round.

With A, knit 1 round, work eyelet round: *k2, yo, k2tog; repeat from *. Knit 1 round.

With B, knit 1 round, working k1b into the yo's.

Section 2 Heel stitch

Round 1 With A, *k1, slip 1 stitch wyib; repeat from *.
Round 2 With B, knit.
Repeat rounds 1–2 for 4", end with a B round.

Section 3 Tweed stitch

Round 1 With A, *slip 1 stitch wyif, k1; repeat from *.
Round 2 With B, knit.
Round 3 With A, *k1, slip 1 stitch wyif; repeat from *.
Round 4 With B, knit.
Repeat rounds 1–4 for 4", end with a B round.

Section 4 Stockinette stitch

Round 1 With A, knit.
Round 2 With B, knit.
Repeat rounds 1–2 for 4", end with a B round.

Section 5 Garter stitch

Round 1 With A, knit.
Round 2 With A, purl.
Round 3 With B, knit.
Round 4 With B, purl.
Repeat rounds 1–4 for 4", end with a B knit round.

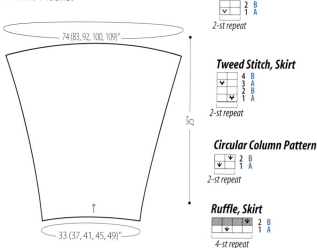

← 74 (83, 92, 100, 109)" →

25"

33 (37, 41, 45, 49)"

→ *Direction of Knitting*

Creating an A-line: each of the first 7 sections of the skirt has a wider gauge than the previous one, even though the needle size and the number of stitches remain constant until the last band when the number of stitches is doubled to form the deep ruffle.

☐ K on RS, p on WS
▨ P on RS
▼ K1b on RS, p1b on RS
▼ P1b on RS
▽ Sl1 with yarn in back
▼ Sl1 with yarn in front

Heel Stitch

| | | 2 | B |
| | | 1 | A |

2-st repeat

Tweed Stitch, Skirt

		4	B
		3	A B A
		2	B
		1	A

2-st repeat

Circular Column Pattern

| | | 2 | B |
| | | 1 | A |

2-st repeat

Ruffle, Skirt

| | | | 2 | B |
| | | | 1 | A |

4-st repeat

Even the waistband section puts the k1b stitch to good use, accentuating and reinforcing the eyelet.

Section 6 Column pattern

Round 1 With A, *k1, k1b; repeat from *.
Round 2 With B, *k1b, k1; repeat from *.
Repeat rounds 1–2 for 4", end with a B round.

Section 7 Ruffle pattern

Increase round With A, *k1, yo, k1b, yo; repeat from * —400 (448, 496, 544, 592) sts. **Next round** With B, purl, purling through the back loop of the yarn-overs.
Round 1 With A, *k2, k1b, k1; repeat from *.
Round 2 With B, *p1b, p3; repeat from *.
Repeat rounds 1–2 for 4", end with a B round. Cut B yarn. With A, *p1, k1, k1b, p1; repeat from *.

Section 8 Sideways garter bind-off

With A, loop cast on 2 stitches onto left needle
Row 1 (RS) P1, p2tog, turn.
Row 2 (WS) P2, turn. Repeat until all stitches have been bound off. Graft last 2 stitches to the two cast-on stitches at the beginning of the round.

Braided cord

Make an 8-foot long, 4-strand braid. Tie overhand knot and trim ends to 1". Feed cord through eyelets, circling waist twice as can be seen on the photograph.

Weaver's Knot

1 Cross the two ends, left over right and hold the junction between the thumb and first finger of the left hand. Take the right yarn around the thumb and pass it behind the left end and bring it to the front.

2 Bend the right-hand end and insert it into the circle as shown.

3 Tighten knot (pulling all 4 strands).

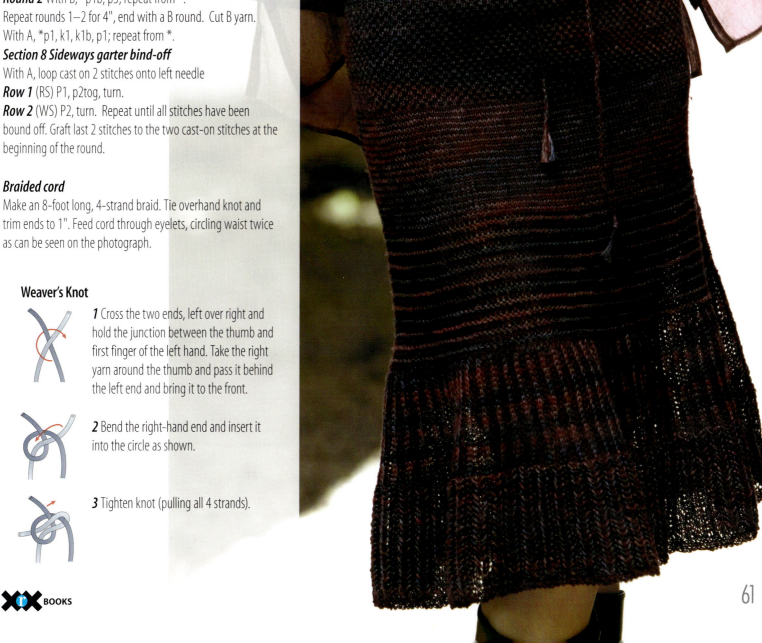

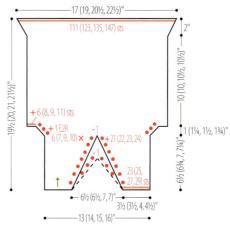

→ *Direction of knitting*

Linen Top

Increase Work M1 increase after first stitch at beginning of row or before last stitch at end of row.

Front

Note for front Color A is variegated, B is solid

Left front

With A and using long-tail loop cast-on, cast on 23 (25, 27, 29) stitches. Join B at tail-end of needle and purl across row (A and B are at same end of needle); turn. ***Shape V-neck*** Work Tweed Stitch, increasing 1 stitch at end of every WS B row (row 4 of pattern) 11 (12, 13, 14) times, then every B row 10 times—44 (47, 50, 53) stitches. End after Row 1. Cut B, do not cut A. Put on hold.

Right front

Using second ball of A, work as for left front EXCEPT increase at beginning of every WS B row 11 (12, 13, 14) times, then every B row 10 times; cut A, do not cut B.

Join fronts, next row (RS B row) Knit to last stitch of right front, knit next stitch together with first stitch of left front, knit remaining stitches from holder—87 (93, 99, 105) stitches. Work until piece measures 6½ (6¾, 7, 7¼)" from cast-on, end with an A row.

Shape armhole Increase 1 stitch at armhole edges every B row 6 (7, 9, 10) times.

Next B row Cast on 6 (8, 9, 11) stitches for each underarm—111 (123, 135, 147) stitches. Work until piece measures 17½ (18, 19, 19½)" from cast-on, end with a WS B row. Work ruffle for 2", end with WS A row. With A, YO bind off in purl.

Back

Note for back Color A is solid, B is variegated

Right back

Pick up 23 (25, 27, 29) stitches from right front shoulder by sliding needle through cast-on loops. With WS facing, join B and purl 1 row; turn. Join A; continue as for Left Front EXCEPT increase at neck edge EVERY B row 21 (22, 23, 24) times, end with a RS A row.

Left back

Work as for right back EXCEPT pick up stitches from left front shoulder. Complete as for front.

Finishing

Sew side seams from underarm to top of ruffle. With the variegated yarn, work 1 round of crab-stitch crochet around the armholes and neck edge.

Tweed Stitch OVER AN ODD NUMBER OF STITCHES

Row 1 (RS) With A, k1, *slip 1 stitch wyif, k1; repeat from*, slide.

Row 2 (RS) With B, knit, turn.

Row 3 (WS) With A, p1, *p1, slip 1 stitch wyib; repeat from *, end p2, slide.

Row 4 (WS) With B, purl, turn.

Repeat rows 1–4 for tweed stitch.

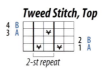

Tweed Stitch, Top

2-st repeat

Ruffle OVER AN ODD NUMBER OF STITCHES

Row 1 (RS) With A, k1, *k1b, k1; repeat from *, slide.

Row 2 (RS) With B, p1, *p1, p1b; repeat from *, end p2, turn.

Row 3 (WS) With A, p1, *p1b, p1; repeat from *, slide.

Row 4 (WS) With B, k1, *k1, k1b; repeat from *, end k2, turn.

Repeat rows 1–4 for Ruffle.

Ruffle, Top

2-st repeat

☐ K on RS, p on WS
▩ P on RS, k on WS
↓ K1b on RS, p1b on RS
↓ P1b on RS
↓ Sl1 with yarn in front on RS, Sl with yarn in back on WS

With its shallow V-neck in the back and deep V-neck in the front, the tank top has a front-to-back option. And reversing Colors A and B for the front and back gives you two looks in one piece.

Garter-stitch edging

All rows Slip 1 stitch with yarn in front, yarn to back, k2; knit last 3 stitches

Wrapskirt

One Size

10cm/4"

34

24

• over stockinette stitch (after hand washing and drying flat)

1 2 3 **4** 5 6

Medium weight

1740 yds

4mm/US 6, or size to obtain gauge, 60cm (24") or longer

&

Tapestry needle

One Size 15 skeins PRISM YARNS Tencel Tape in color Thunderclap

Notes

1 See Techniques, page 138, for long-tail loop cast-on, k1b, p1b, sl 1 wyif, sl1 wyib, and slide.
2 Slip all stitches as if to purl.

Using long-tail loop cast-on, cast on 275 stitches (an odd number), turn. Knit 1 row.

Skirt
Section 1 Upper edging
Row 1 (RS) *K1, slip 1 with yarn in back (sl 1 wyib); repeat from *, end k1.
Row 2 (WS) *Sl 1 wyib, k1; repeat from *, end sl 1 wyib.
Work rows 1–2 a total of 4 times.

Slipping first stitch and knitting next 2 and last 3 stitches of all rows, work center 269 stitches in following 9 patterns:

Section 2 Offset heel stitch
Row 1 (RS) *Sl 1 wyib, k1; repeat from *, end sl 1.
Rows 2 and 4 (WS) Purl.
Row 3 (RS) *K1, sl 1 wyib; repeat from *, end k1.
Repeat rows 1–4 for 2".

Section 3 Tweed stitch
Row 1 (RS) *K1, slip 1 with yarn in front (sl 1 wyif); repeat from *, end k1.
Rows 2 and 4 (WS) Purl.
Row 3 (RS) *Sl 1 wyif, k1; repeat from *, end sl 1 wyif.
Repeat rows 1–4 for 2¼".

Section 4 Stockinette stitch
Row 1 (RS) Knit.
Row 2 (WS) Purl.
Repeat rows 1–2 for 2½".

Section 5 Garter stitch
All rows Purl.
Work for 2¾".

Section 6 K1b stitch
Row 1 (RS) *K1b, k1; repeat from *, end k1b.
Row 2 (WS) *P1, p1b; repeat from *, end p1.
Repeat rows 1–2 for 3".

Section 7 Reverse k1b stitch
Row 1 (RS) *P1, p1b; repeat from *, end p1.
Row 2 (WS) *K1b, k1; repeat from *, end k1b.
Repeat rows 1–2 for 3¼".

Section 8 Two-sided k1b pattern
Row 1 (RS) *K1b, k1; repeat from *, end k1b.
Row 2 (WS) *K1, k1b; repeat from *, end k1.
Repeat rows 1–2 for 3½".

Section 9 Ruffle
Set-up row 1 (RS) *Yo, k1b, yo, k1; repeat from *, end yo, k1b, yo—545 stitches, including edge stitches.
Set-up row 2 (WS) Knit all stitches, knitting yos through back loop to avoid holes.
Row 1 (RS) *K1, k1b, k2; repeat from *, end k1, k1b, k1.
Row 2 (WS) *K3, k1b; repeat from *, end k3.
Repeat rows 1–2 for 4", ending after Row 1.

Section 10 Sideways garter bind-off
Set-up row (WS) *K1, p1, k1, k1b; repeat from *, end k3. With (RS) facing, cast 2 stitches onto left needle
Row 1 P1, p2tog, turn.
Row 2 P2, turn. Repeat rows 1–2 until 2 stitches remain. Pull the right stitch over the left stitch. Cut yarn and pull end of yarn through loop.
Sew in ends.
Wrap and fasten with a pin.

Offset heel stitch

2-st repeat

Tweed stitch

2-st repeat

K1b stitch

2-st repeat

Reverse k1b stitch

2-st repeat

Two-sided k1b pattern

2-st repeat

Ruffle

4-st repeat

☐ K on RS, p on WS
▨ P on RS, k on WS
⤵ K1b on RS, p1b on WS
⤵ P1b on RS, k1b on WS
⤵ Sl1 with yarn in front on RS, Sl1 with yarn in back on WS

The skirt swings from the double-knit waistband, with gradually widening tiers that drape elegantly.

Column Pattern OVER AN ODD NUMBER OF STITCHES
Row 1 (RS) With A, k1, *k1b, k1; repeat from *, slide.
Row 2 (RS) With B, k1, *k1, k1b; repeat from *, end k2, turn.
Row 3 (WS) With A, p1, *p1b, p1; repeat from *, slide.
Row 4 (WS) With B, p1, *p1, p1b; repeat from *, end p2, turn.
Repeat rows 1–4 for Column Pattern.

Column Pattern

2-st repeat

☐ K on RS, p on WS
▼ K1b on RS, p1b on WS

T-V Top

INTERMEDIATE

OVERSIZED FIT

XS–S (M–L, 1X–2X)
A 43 (50, 57)"
B 20½ (22½, 24½)"
C 20 (21, 22)"

10cm/4"

48
14
• **over Column Pattern**

1 **2** 3 4 5 6
Fine weight

A & B • 425 (525, 625) yds each

3.25 mm/US 3 (24"), or size to
obtain gauge
Extra needle for 3-needle bind-off

&

Stitch holders and yarn needle

XS-Small: 2 balls each SKACEL-
SCHULANA Kid-Seta in color 16 Teal
(A) and #19 Magenta (B)

Notes

1 See *Techniques*, page 138, for loop cast-on, long-tail loop cast-on, k1b, p1b, p2tog, kf&b, pf&b, 3-needle YO bind-off, p2tog bind-off, and slide. *2* The body and sleeve rectangles are worked from the top down. *3* Back triangle is worked in 3-row stripes; carry color not in use up sides. Use a coilless safety pin or stitch marker to mark RS of back triangle.

Border

Knit 1 row, purl 1 row, knit 1 row. With RS facing and loop cast-on, cast 1 stitch onto needle.
Row 1 (RS) P2tog (1 edging stitch together with 1 sleeve or body stitch), turn.
Row 2 (WS) P1, turn.
Repeat rows 1–2 across all stitches. Fasten off.

Sleeves

With A and using long-tail loop cast-on, cast on 55 (63, 71) stitches. Join B at tail-end of needle and purl across row (A and B are at same end of needle), turn. Work Column Pattern until piece measures approximately 19 (20, 21)" from beginning, end with a RS B row (row 2 of pattern). With B, work Border.
Upper sleeve border With RS facing and A, pick up and knit 1 stitch in each column across top of sleeve. Work Border.

Body rectangles MAKE 2

With A and using long-tail loop cast-on, cast on 72 (84, 96) stitches. Join B at tail-end of needle and purl across row (A and B are at same end of needle); turn. Work 2×2 Column Pattern until piece measures approximately 12 (13, 14)" from beginning, end with a RS B row. With B, work Border.
Side borders With RS facing and B, pick up and knit 2 stitches for every 3 Vs along side of rectangle. Work Border. Repeat on other side of rectangle.

Back triangle

Notes 1 Turn work at end of row unless told to slide. *2* For increase rows, kf&b on RS, pf&b on WS.
With A and using loop cast-on, cast on 3 stitches; purl 1 row (RS), knit 1 row.
Increase row (RS) With B, kf&b, knit to last stitch, kf&b, turn—2 stitches increased.
With B, purl 1 row, knit 1 row, slide.

2×2 Column Pattern MULTIPLE OF 4 STITCHES

Row 1 (RS) With A, k1, *k2, k1b, k1b; repeat from *, end k3, slide.
Row 2 (RS) With B, k1, *k1b, k1b, k2; repeat from *, end k1b, k1b, k1, turn.
Row 3 (WS) With A, p1, *p2, p1b, p1b; repeat from *, end p3, slide.
Row 4 (WS) With B, p1, *p1b, p1b, p2; repeat from *, end p1b, p1b, p1, turn.
Repeat rows 1–4 for 2×2 Column Pattern.

2 × 2 Column Pattern

4-st repeat

* With A, purl 1 row, knit 1 row, purl 1 row.
With B, work WS increase row, knit 1 row, purl 1 row, slide.
With A, knit 1 row, purl 1 row, knit 1 row.
With B, work RS increase row, purl 1 row, knit 1 row, slide.
Repeat from * 4 (5, 6) times more—25 (29, 33) stitches.
Edging With A, (purl 1 row, knit 1 row) 2 times.
With RS facing and A, bind off using p2tog bind-off.

Finishing

Place markers along side borders of sleeves, approximately 10 (10½, 11)" from top.

Join sleeves to body With RS facing and A, pick up and knit 1 stitch for each column across top edge of one of the body rectangles—72 (84, 96) stitches. With RS facing, extra needle, and A, pick up and knit 36 (42, 48) stitches between marker and cast-on edge of one sleeve and the same number between cast-on edge and marker on right edge of other sleeve—72 (84, 96) stitches. With WS together and beginning at underarm, work 3-needle YO bind-off across to join body and sleeves. Join other body rectangle to other edge of sleeves.

Join sleeve seams With RS facing and A, pick up and knit 2 stitches for every 3 visible rows along one side of sleeve. Pick up and knit same number of stitches down other side of same sleeve. With WS together, work 3-needle YO bind-off. Join other sleeve seam.

Sew side seams for 3" or desired length from underarm. Sew triangle in space between sleeve top edges in back, working beneath sleeve border so it covers seam.

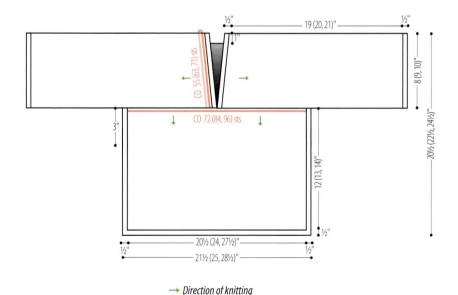

→ *Direction of knitting*

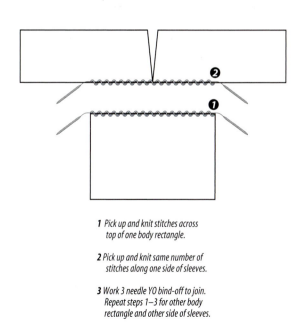

1 Pick up and knit stitches across top of one body rectangle.

2 Pick up and knit same number of stitches along one side of sleeves.

3 Work 3 needle YO bind-off to join. Repeat steps 1–3 for other body rectangle and other side of sleeves.

T-V Top

Columns of different widths are an eye-catching element of the diaphanous top, which floats lightly with its open side seams.

Offset Tabard

A longer version would fashion an elegant and flowing garment—just work a few inches more before shaping the armholes. The sloping shoulder, made with short rows, are easy to work and virtually invisible in the Column Pattern.

Column Pattern 1 (2) (OVER AN ODD NUMBER OF STITCHES)
Row 1 (RS) With B (A), k1, * k1b, k1; repeat from *, slide.
Row 2 (RS) With A (B), k1, * k1, k1b; repeat from *, end k2, turn.
Row 3 (WS) With B (A), p1, * p1b, p1; repeat from *, slide.
Row 4 (WS) With A (B), p1, * p1, p1b; repeat from *, end p2, turn.

Column Pattern 1

Column Pattern 2

Offset Tabard

INTERMEDIATE

LOOSE FIT
Size S (M, L, 1X)
A · 41½ (45½, 49½, 53½)"
B · 18 (19, 20, 21)"

10cm/4"
48
16
· *over Column Pattern*

Light Weight
A · 400 (450, 525, 600) yds
B · 350 (400, 450, 500) yds

3.5mm/US 4, or size to obtain
gauge, 40cm (16") and 60cm (24")
or longer
Extra needle for 3-needle bind-off

Stitch holders and yarn needle

Small: 3 balls each ALPACA WITH
A TWIST Punch! in color 0500 Black
Pearl (A) and 3012 Cherry (B)

Note
See *Techniques*, page 138, for long-tail loop cast-on, k1b, p1b, I-cord, k2tog, sl 1 pwise, 3-needle YO bind-off, and slide.

Back
With longer circular needle, A, and using long-tail loop cast-on, cast on 83 (91, 99, 107) stitches.
Join B at end of needle opposite A tail and knit across row (A and B are now at opposite ends of the needle), slide. *Next row* With A, purl, turn. Work Column Pattern 1 beginning with row 1 until piece measures approximately 1¾", end with a WS A row. Work even in Column Pattern 2 until piece measures approximately 9 (9½, 10, 10½)", end with a RS A row.
Shape right armhole
YO bind off 6 (7, 8, 8) stitches at beginning of next row (RS B row), then k2tog at beginning of RS B rows 6 (7, 8, 8) times—71 (77, 83, 91) stitches. Work even until armhole measures approximately 6½ (7, 7½, 8)", end with a WS B row.
Back short-row shaping
RS row 1 With A, work to 4 (4, 6, 8) stitches from end of row (stop just before A column), slide. Place remaining 4 (4, 6, 8) stitches on hold. *RS row 2* Work across with B, turn. *WS row 3* With A, slip 1 stitch purlwise (sl 1), work to end, slide. *WS row 4* With B, slip 1 stitch purlwise (sl 1), work to end, *RS row 5* Work across to last 4 stitches and place those 4 stitches on hold with other currently held stitches. *RS row 6* Work across with B. *WS row 7* Sl1, work to end. *WS row 8* Sl 1, work to end. Repeat last 4 rows 6 times more—39 (45, 49, 55) stitches. *Next 2 rows* Work across all stitches on needle and holder.

Front
Work as Back to underarm, end with a WS A row.
Shape right armhole
YO bind off 6 (7, 8, 8) stitches at beginning of next row (WS B row) then SSK at end of every RS B row 6 (7, 8, 8) times—71 (77, 83, 91) stitches. Work even until armhole measures approximately 6 (6½, 7, 7½)", end with a WS B row.

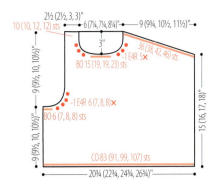

Diagram labels:
2½ (2½, 3, 3)"
10 (10, 12, 12) sts
6 (7¼, 7¼, 8¼)"
9 (9¾, 10½, 11½)"
3"
36 (38, 42, 46) sts
-1 E4R 5✗
BO 15 (19, 19, 23) sts
9 (9½, 10, 10½)"
15 (16, 17, 18)"
-1 E4R 6 (7, 8, 8)✗
BO 6 (7, 8, 8) sts
9 (9½, 10, 10½)"
CO 83 (91, 99, 107) sts
20¾ (22¾, 24¾, 26¾)"

Shape neck

RS row 1 With A, work across all 71 (77, 83, 91) stitches. **RS row 2** With B, work 41 (43, 47, 51) stitches, YO bind off 15 (19,19, 23) stitches, work 15 (15, 17, 17) stitches.

WS row 3 WORKING BOTH SIDES AT SAME TIME With A, work 15 (15, 17, 17) stitches, join 2nd ball of A and work across 41 (43, 47, 51) stitches, slide. **WS row 4** With B, work 15 (15, 17, 17) stitches, join 2nd ball of B and work across 41 (43, 47, 51) stitches, turn. **RS row 5** With A, work across decreasing 1 stitch at each neck edge, slide. **RS row 6** With B, work even, turn. **WS rows 7, 8** Work 2 rows even. **RS row 9** With A, work across decreasing 1 stitch at each edge of neck, slide. **RS row 10** With B, work across, turn. **WS row 11** With A, work across to last 4 (4, 6, 8) stitches, place remaining 4 (4, 6, 8) stitches on hold, slide. **WS row 12** With B, work across, turn. **RS row 13** With A, sl1, work across decreasing 1 st each side of neck, slide. **RS row 14** With B, sl 1, work across, turn. **WS row 15** With A, work across to last 4 stitches and place those 4 stitches on hold, slide.

Rows 16–23 Repeat last 4 rows twice more. **WS row 24** With B work even, turn. **RS row 25** With A, sl1, work across, slide. **RS row 26** With B, sl 1, work across, turn. **WS row 27** With A, work across to last 4 stitches, place them on hold, slide. **Rows 28–39** Repeat last 4 rows 3 times more. **WS row 40** With B, sl1, work across turn. **RS row 41** With A, sl1, work across, slide. **RS row 42** With B, sl1, work across, turn. **WS row 43** With A, work across all stitches on needle, and holder. Leave stitches on needle. Do not cut A.

Finishing

Join shoulders Work 3-needle YO bind-off to join 36 (38, 42, 46) stitches of left shoulder, continue across back neck with a normal bind-off (without YOs) until 10 (10, 12, 12) stitches remain. Join right shoulder with 3-needle YO bind-off.

Join right side seam With RS facing and A, begin at the bottom of front and pick up and knit 2 stitches for every 3 Vs along right side edge. At the color shift, change to B for the rest of the edge. With a second needle, repeat pick up along right side edge of back. With WS together, join with 3-needle YO bind-off, working in same color as the picked-up stitches.

Armhole edging With RS facing, 16" circular needle, and A, begin at underarm and pick up and knit 2 stitches for every 3 Vs along the vertical edge, 1 stitch for each column along diagonal edge, and 3 stitches for every 2 columns across the horizontal edge.

Work 3-stitch I-cord edging as follows: Loop cast on 3 stitches, *k2, k2tog (I-cord stitch together with edging stitch), slip stitches back to left needle; repeat from *.

Neck edging Work same as armhole edging, beginning at right shoulder and picking up and knitting 3 stitches for every 2 columns across back of neck, 2 stitches for every 3 Vs along vertical edge, 1 stitch for each column along diagonal edge, and 3 stitches for every 2 columns along front neck bind-off.

Left side edging With RS facing, 24" circular needle, and A, pick up 1 stitch for each V along left side of front and back. With 16" circular needle and A, make 25" of 3-stitch I-cord for the first tie; continue, working I-cord edging along picked-up stitches; then work I-cord for another 25" for tie.

Bind off and sew in ends.

Circular Column Pattern OVER AN EVEN NUMBER OF STITCHES
Round 1 With A, *k1b, k1; repeat from *.
Round 2 With B, *k1, k1b; repeat from *.
Repeat rounds 1–2 for Circular Column Pattern.

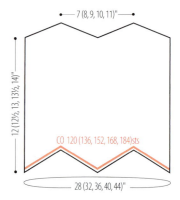

Circular Column Pattern

2 B
1 A

2-st repeat

☐ Knit
⤓ K1b

Chevron Camisole

INTERMEDIATE

VERY CLOSE FIT

XS (S, M, L, 1X)
A 28 (32, 36, 40, 44)" around
B 12 (12½, 13, 13½, 14)" to strap

10cm/4"

48
16

• For convenience, work a back-and-forth swatch over Column Pattern on page 4

1 2 **3** 4 5 6

Light weight
A & B • 210 (250, 300, 350, 400) yds each

3.5mm/US 4, 60cm (24") long, or size to obtain gauge.

Stitch markers and yarn needle

Small: 2 skeins each FIESTA La Luz in color #3319 Cactus Bloom (A) and La Luz Multi in color # 17146 Cosmopolitan (B)

Note

See *Techniques*, page 138, for double loop cast-on, k1b, S2KP2, double increase, and knit loop bind-off.

Camisole

With A and using double loop cast-on, cast on 120 (136, 152, 168, 184) stitches. Continuing with single yarn, purl 1 row. Join; mark beginning of round. Knit one round.
Begin Chevron Pattern: Rounds 1, 3 With A, *k1b, k1; repeat from *.
Rounds 2, 4 With B, *k1, k1b; repeat from *.
Round 5 With A, remove marker, k1b, replace marker (marker moves one stitch to the left); *[k1, k1b] 6 (7, 8, 9, 10) times, k1, work double increase, [k1, k1b] 6 (7, 8, 9, 10) times, k1, S2KP2, repeat from * 4 times.
Rounds 6, 8 With B, *k1b, k1; repeat from *.
Rounds 7, 9 With A, *k1, k1b; repeat from *.
Round 10 With B, work as for Round 5.
Repeat last 10 rounds until piece measures approximately 12 (12½, 13, 13½, 14)" or to desired length, end with Round 9. With A, purl 1 round and bind off using knit loop bind-off.

Straps MAKE 2

With B, cast on 3 stitches. *Slip 1 with yarn in front, take yarn to back, k2; turn. Repeat from * until strap is 14", or desired length. Bind off.

Finishing

Sew one end of strap to camisole at point A and safety pin other end to camisole at point B (see illustration). Repeat for other strap with points C and D. Try on, adjust length of strap, then sew to camisole at B and D.

7 (8, 9, 10, 11)"

12 (12½, 13, 13½, 14)"

CO 120 (136, 152, 168, 184)sts

28 (32, 36, 40, 44)"

This camisole is knit in the round and the bias fabric hugs the figure. The subtle coloring of the yarns de-emphasizes the columns, while the stitch pattern comes to the fore with its diagonal lines.

Column Pattern with Beads OVER ODD NUMBER OF STITCHES
Row 1 (RS) With A, knit all stitches, slide.
Row 2 (RS) With B, k1, *k1b, k1; repeat from *, turn.
Row 3 (WS) With A, p1, *p1, p1b; repeat from * ending p2, slide.
Row 4 (WS) With B, p1, *p1b, p1; repeat from *, turn.
Row 5 (RS) With A, k1, *k1, k1b; repeat from * ending k2, slide.
Row 6 (RS) With B, k1, *k1b, k1; repeat from *, turn.
Row 7 (WS) With A, k1, *place bead, k1; repeat from *, slide.
Row 8 (WS) With B, p1, *place bead, p1; repeat from *, turn.
Repeat Rows 1-8 for Column Pattern with Beads.

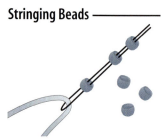

Column Pattern with Beads

2-st repeat

☐ K on RS, p on WS
▨ K on WS
☑ K1b on RS, p1b on WS
◉ Place bead between 2 stitches

Beaded Necklace

10cm/4"
108
32
• over Pattern Stitch
with beads

1 2 3 4 5 6
Super fine weight

A & B • 85 yds each

Two 1.5mm/US 000,
or size to obtain gauge

&

Sewing needle, beading needle,
and Size 10/11 seed beads (1 hank,
approximately 2000)

1 ball each DMC #8 Pearl Cotton in dark
pink (A) and light pink (B)

Notes
1 See Techniques, page 138, for long-tail loop cast-on, k1b, p1b, overhand knot, and slide.
2 Tighten edge stitches as you work.

Preparation
Using beading needle, string approximately 800 beads each onto A and B threads (more for a longer necklace).

Holder
With A and using long-tail loop cast-on, cast on 21 stitches, turn. [With A, k1, *bring bead to needle (place bead), k1; repeat from * to end of row, slide; with B, p1, *place bead, p1; repeat from * to end of row, turn] 2 times. Work Column Pattern with Beads for 3" or desired length, end with Row 5 of pattern. Cut both yarns and thread each through the live stitches to opposite end of needle, pull tight and secure. Sew side seam of holder, sew in ends.

Strap
With Color A or B and using long-tail loop cast-on, cast on 4 stitches, turn. **Every row** K1, *place bead, k1; repeat from *, turn. Work for 30" or desired length. Sew strap onto holder, covering the side seam with one end of the strap.

Tassel
String 600 beads onto B; cut twenty 12" lengths, each with 30 beads on it. The bead closest to the beading needle will be the turning bead; pull needle back through 29 beads above it. Equalize thread lengths. Repeat for all 12" lengths of thread. Using an overhand knot, tie 5 lengths together directly above the beads. Repeat with remaining lengths, 4 bundles total. Thread the ends of the bundles into the bottom of the holder; secure by tying them together.

Stringing Beads

Using a beading needle, string 800 beads on A and B.

Placing Beads

After knitting a stitch, bring bead to needle before knitting next stitch.

Want to carry a cell phone or an MP3 player? Just add more stitches and beads. Or pick a heavier yarn and larger beads. Sock yarn and size 6 beads would be a great choice here.

Creature Comforts

84

Merging the sheen of ribbon, the glitz of beads and the warmth of mohair, the **Bo Jangles Shawl** will embrace you in elegance.

78

The openwork fabric of the **Gossamer Square** reveals the diagonal strands that link the columns.

82

86

A slinky tassel swings gracefully from the back of the asymmetrical **Checkmark Scarf**.

The **Mitered Squares Pillow** illustrates yet another technique that can benefit from the k1b stitch.

Circular Column Pattern
Round 1 With A, *k1, k1b; repeat from *.
Round 2 With B, *k1b, k1; repeat from *.

Gossamer Square

40" square,
including edging

10cm/4"
40

12
• over Column Pattern
• For convenience, work gauge
swatch back and forth, following
Column Pattern on page 4

1 2 **3** 4 5 6

Light weight
A & B • 450 yds each

5mm/US 8, or size to obtain
gauge, 60cm (24") or longer
Optional 40cm (16") needle

Five 5mm/US 8

5mm/H-8

Tapestry needle and stitch
markers in 2 colors

One Size: 2 balls each ROWAN Kidsilk
Haze in color 2605 Smoke (A) and Kidsilk
Night in color 608 Moonlight (B)

Notes

1 See *Techniques*, page 138, for long-tail loop cast-on, double increase, k1b, and working with dpns. *2* Do not twist yarns when changing colors at the end of the round. Work color change loosely. *3* Change to circular needle when necessary, placing marker at end of each needle and different-colored marker at end of the round. *4* Where necessary to maintain color of columns, insert crochet hook 1 below stitch on needle.

Shawl

With A, a double-pointed needle (dpn), and using long-tail loop cast-on, cast on 8 stitches. Join B at tail-end of needle and knit across row (A and B are at same end of needle). Distribute stitches over 4 dpn, with 2 stitches on each. Join and mark beginning of round. Work 2 rounds in Column Pattern.

Increase round 3 With A, *work **1** stitch in pattern, double increase; repeat from *—**16** stitches.

Round 4 and all even-numbered rounds With B, *k1b, k1; repeat from *.

Rounds 5, 9, and all non-increase, odd-numbered rounds With A, *k1, k1b; repeat from *.

Increase round 7 Work **1** stitch in pattern before double increase—**24** stitches.

Continue to increase 8 stitches every 4th round.

Round 11 Work **3** stitches in pattern before double increase—**32** stitches.

Round 15 Work **3** stitches before double increase—**40** stitches.

Round 19 Work **5** stitches—**48** stitches. **Round 23** Work **5** stitches—**56** stitches.

Round 27 Work **7** stitches—**64** stitches. **Round 31** Work **7** stitches—**72** stitches.

Round 35 Work **9** stitches—**80** stitches. **Round 39** Work **9** stitches—**88** stitches.

Round 43 Work **11** stitches—**96** stitches. **Round 47** Work **11** stitches—**104** stitches.

Round 51 Work **13** stitches—**112** stitches. **Round 55** Work **13** stitches—**120** stitches.

Round 59 Work **15** stitches—**128** stitches. **Round 63** Work **15** stitches—**136** stitches.

Round 67 Work **17** stitches—**144** stitches. **Round 71** Work **17** stitches—**152** stitches. Etc.

When shawl is desired size, end with a B round. Do not cut yarns.

Work edging, block shawl, pinning out the crochet loops.

Each scallop 'grows' out of the matching column, producing an organic edging that does not look tacked on. Twisting the spiraling chains calls for a bit of patience, so choose your favorite way of holding the out-of-work chains, put on some good music, and crochet away.

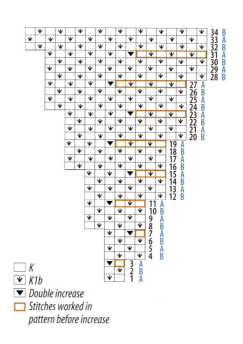

Legend:

- ☐ K
- ⬇ K1b
- ▼ Double increase
- ▢ Stitches worked in pattern before increase

Edging (spiraling chain crochet bind-off) Place next B stitch on crochet hook and chain 6 with B, place chain on a holder (for example, a cable needle, split ring stitch marker, or coilless safety pin) and drop to back of work. Place next A stitch onto hook and chain 6 with A, place that chain on a second holder and drop to back of work. *Place stitch from 1st holder on hook. With B, sc into next B stitch and chain 5, place on holder. Place stitch from 2nd holder on hook. With A, sc into next A stitch and chain 5, place on holder. Continue from * until all stitches are worked. End final B chain by placing stitch on hook, slip stitch into original B stitch of crochet round. Fasten off. Repeat for A. Fasten off. Secure ends.

Gossamer Square

A haze of columns will surround you when you drape this shawl over your shoulders.

Checkmark Scarf

Is it a scarf? Is it a shawl? With the differing widths and lengths of its two sections, the Checkmark Scarf can be worn either way.

INTERMEDIATE

10cm/4"

30

10

• over Column Pattern
• For convenience, work gauge swatch back and forth, following Column Pattern on page 4

1 2 3 **4** 5 6

Medium weight
A • 230 yds
B • 165 yds

5mm/US 8, or size to obtain gauge, 60cm/24" long

H/5mm

&

Tapestry needle

Gold Scarf: 1 ball each FIESTA Gelato in color 3141 Malibu (A) and La Boheme in color 2553 Cajeta (B)
Pink Scarf: 1 ball each FIESTA Gelato in color 3145 White Zinfandel (A) and La Boheme in color 2501 Petal Pink (B)

Checkmark Scarf

Notes

1 See *Techniques*, page 138, for long-tail loop cast-on, kf&b, k1b, p1b, k2tog, SSK, slide, YO bind-off, single crochet, chain, and tassel. *2* When two numbers are given, the first is for the gold scarf, the number in parenthesis is for the pink scarf. If there is only one number, it applies to both scarves.

Scarf

With A and using long-tail loop cast-on, cast on 27 (33) stitches. Join B at tail-end of needle and purl across row (both A and B are now at same end of needle); turn.

Section 1

Row 1 (RS) With A, k2tog, *k1, k1b; repeat from *, end kf&b, slide.
Row 2 (RS) With B, k1 *k1b, k1; repeat from *, turn.
Row 3 (WS) With A, p1, *p1, p1b; repeat from *, end p2, slide.
Row 4 (WS) With B, p1 *p1b, p1; repeat from •, turn.
Row 5 (RS) With A, k2tog, *k1b, k1; repeat from *, end kf&b, slide.
Row 6 (RS) With B, k1 *k1, k1b; repeat from *, end k2, turn.
Row 7 (WS) With A, p1 *p1b, p1; repeat from *, slide.
Row 8 (WS) With B, p1 *p1, p1b; repeat from *, end p2, turn.
Continue this 8-row repeat until half of A has been used and work measures approximately 42 (32)", end with row 8.

Section 2

Row 1 (RS) With A, kf&b, *k1b, k1; repeat from *, end k1b, kf&b, slide—2 stitches increased.
Row 2 (RS) With B, k1 *k1b, k1; repeat from *, turn.
Row 3 (WS) With A, p1, *p1, p1b; repeat from *, end p2, slide.
Row 4 (WS) With B, p1 *p1b, p1; repeat from *, turn.
Row 5 (RS) With A, kf&b, *k1, k1b; repeat from *, end k1, kf&b, slide—2 stitches increased.
Row 6 (RS) With B, k1, * k1, k1b; repeat from *, end k2, turn.
Row 7 (WS) With A, p1 *p1b, p1; repeat from *, slide.
Row 8 (WS) With B, p1 *p1, p1b; repeat from *, end p2, turn.
Each 8-row repeat of Section 2 increases stitch count by 4. Work a total of 3 (1½) repeats of Section 2—39 stitches.

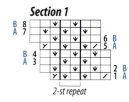

Section 1

2-st repeat

Section 2

2-st repeat

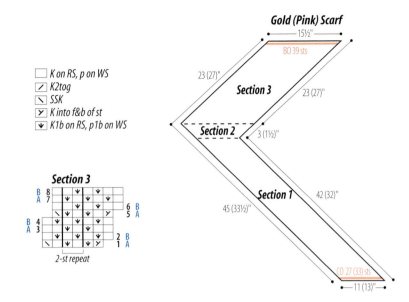

Gold (Pink) Scarf

15½"
BO 39 sts
23 (27)"
Section 3
23 (27)"
Section 2
3 (1½)"
Section 1
42 (32)"
45 (33½)"
CO 27 (33) sts
11 (13)"

☐ K on RS, p on WS
⟋ K2tog
⟍ SSK
⎐ K into f&b of st
⤓ K1b on RS, p1b on WS

Section 3

8
B 7
A
6 B
5 A
B 4
A 3
2 B
1 A

2-st repeat

Section 3

Row 1 (RS) With A, kf&b, *k1b, k1; repeat from *, end SSK, slide.

Row 2 (RS) With B, k1 *k1b, k1; repeat from *, turn.

Row 3 (WS) With A, p1, *p1, p1b; repeat from *, end p2, slide.

Row 4 (WS) With B, p1 *p1b, p1; repeat from *, turn.

Row 5 (RS) With A, kf&b, *k1, k1b; repeat from *, end SSK, slide.

Row 6 (RS) With B, k1, *k1, k1b; repeat from *, end k2, turn.

Row 7 (WS) With A, p1 *p1b, p1; repeat from *, slide.

Row 8 (WS) With B, p1, *p1, p1b; repeat from *, end p2, turn.

Continue this 8-row repeat until there is no more B or scarf is desired length, end with row 4 or row 8.

With RS facing, YO bind off with A, pull ball of yarn through last loop. Do not cut A.

Finishing

With RS facing, crochet hook, and A, work edging on the bias edges (long sides) as follows: *work 1 single crochet (sc), chain (ch) 2; repeat from * , working the sc into the scarf every 4th row. Work edging on the cast-on and bind-off edges (short ends) as follows: *work 1 sc, ch1; repeat from * across the ends, working the sc into the V of each column of stitches. Sew in ends. Stretch to block and steam. Make a tassel with A and attach to the point at back.

Peak-and-Valley Pattern OVER AN ODD NUMBER OF STITCHES
Row 1 (RS) With A, k1, *k1b, k1; repeat from *, slide.
Row 2 (RS) With B, p1, *p1, p1b; repeat from *, end p2, turn.
Row 3 (WS) With A, p1, *p1b, p1; repeat from *, slide.
Row 4 (WS) With B, k1, *k1, k1b; repeat from *, end k2, turn.
Repeat rows 1–4 for Peak-and-Valley Pattern.

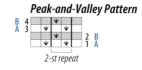

Peak-and-Valley Pattern

2-st repeat

☐ K on RS, p on WS
▨ P on RS, k on WS
☑ K1b on RS, p1b on WS
☑ P1b on RS, k1b on WS

Bo Jangles Shawl

Notes
1 See *Techniques*, page 138, for long-tail loop cast-on, k1b, p1b, knit loop bind-off, purl loop bind-off, and slide.
2 Since you may want to bind off with A or with B, we have given you instructions for both.

Shawl
With A and using long-tail loop cast-on, cast on 125 stitches. Join B at tail-end of needle and knit across row (A and B are at same end of needle), turn. Work Peak-and-Valley Pattern until shawl measures approximately 14" from beginning.
For bind-off in color A End with a WS B row. **Next row** (RS) With A, p1, *k1b, p1; repeat from *, turn. With WS facing and A, bind off using purl loop bind-off.
Or for bind-off in color B End with a WS A row. **Next row** (WS) With B, k1, *p1, k1b; end k1, p1, turn. With RS facing and B, bind off using knit loop bind-off.
Block. Sew beads to the ends, if desired, saving a few for a matching pair of earrings!

EASY

14" x 50"
(without fringe)

10cm/4"

34

10

• over Column Pattern
• For convenience, work gauge swatch back and forth, following Column Pattern on page 4

1 2 **3-4** 5 6

Light-Medium weight

A & B • 200 yds each

5.5mm/US 9, or size to obtain gauge, 60cm (24") or longer

&

Stitch holders , yarn needle
Optional: Large decorative beads, 5mm beads, beading thread, beading needle, earring hooks

One Size: 2 skeins each Mohair blend (A) ANNY BLATT Rayon Ribbon in color 749 Beryl (B)

On one side, the ribbon forms 'peaks' with the mohair in the 'valleys.' The opposite side has mohair 'peaks' and ribbon 'valleys.'

84

→ *Direction of work*
— *Cast on*
---- *pick up and knit*

Mitered Squares Pillow

INTERMEDIATE

Approximately
12" x 12", before border

10cm/4"

42

12

• over Column Pattern, using
larger needle
• For convenience, work gauge
swatch back and forth, following
Column Pattern on page 4

1 2 3 4 **5** 6

Bulky weight

A & B • 150 yds each

C • 75 yds

4mm/US 6 and 4.5mm/US 7, or size
to obtain gauge, (24") or longer
Extra circular needle for 3-needle
bind-off

Seven • 25mm (1")

Stitch holders, yarn needle,
pillow form

2 skeins each TAHKI • FILATURA DI
CROSA, 127 Print in color 54 Red Print
(A) and color 53 Denim Print (B); 1
skein Zara Plus in color 417 Rust (C)

Notes

1 See *Techniques*, page 138, for long-tail loop cast-on, loop
cast-on, k1b, p1b, S2KP2, SSK, SSP, and p2tog bind-off. *2* Work
mitered square in order of numbers on diagrams. *3* Pick up
stitches in the ditch between first 2 stitches. *4* Pick up all stitches
with right side facing.

2-yarn K1b Mitered Square OVER A MULTIPLE OF 8+1 STITCHES
Note Mark center stitch. Begin all squares with WS row 7:
Row 1 (RS) With A, slip 1, *k1, k1b; repeat from *, end k2, slide.
Decrease Row 2 (RS) With B, slip 1, *k1b, k1; repeat from * until 1 stitch
before center stitch, work S2KP2, k1, **k1b, k1; repeat from **, turn.
Row 3 (WS) With A, slip 1, *p1, p1b; repeat from *, end p2, slide.
Row 4 (WS) With B, slip 1, *p1b, p1; repeat from *, turn.
Decrease Row 5 (RS) With A, slip 1, *k1, k1b; repeat from * until
2 stitches before center stitch, k1, work S2KP2, **k1, k1b; repeat
from **, end k2, slide.
Row 6 (RS) With B, slip 1, *k1b, k1; repeat from *, turn.
Row 7 (WS) With A, slip 1 purlwise (slip 1), *p1, p1b; repeat
from *, end p2, slide.
Row 8 (WS) With B, slip 1, *p1b, p1; repeat from *, turn.
Repeat rows 1–8; until 7 stitches remain, end with row 4, turn.
Decrease row With A, slip 1, k1, S2KP2, k2, slide. Work 4 rows in
pattern. *Decrease row* With B, slip 1, S2KP2, k1, turn. **Next row**
With A, slip 1, p2, turn. **Next row** With A, S2KP2. This last stitch will be
the first stitch of the next mitered square.

First Side

Square 1

With larger circular needle, A, and using long-tail loop cast-on, cast
on 25 stitches. Join B at tail end of needle and knit across row (A and
B are at same end of needle); turn. Work 2-yarn K1b Mitered Square.

Square 2, 3

With last stitch of previous square on needle and A, pick up and knit
12 stitches along top of previous square; using loop cast-on, cast
on 12 stitches—25 stitches, slide. With B, knit all stitches; turn.
Work 2-yarn K1b Mitered Square. After Square 3, cut yarns, pull tail
through last stitch.

Square 4, 7

With A, using loop cast-on, cast on 12 stitches, pick up and knit 13
stitches along right edge of completed square. Join B at tail end of
needle and knit across row (A and B are at same end of needle); turn.
Work 2-yarn K1b Mitered Square.

Square 5, 6, 8, 9

With last stitch of previous square on needle and A, pick up and
knit 11 stitches along top of previous square, 1 stitch in the corner,
12 stitches along square to left—25 stitches, slide. With B, knit
all stitches; turn. Work 2-yarn K1b Mitered Square. After squares 6
and 9, cut yarns.

ORIENTATION TIP The stitch before the
S2KP2 is always a k1. That is a good way
to tell whether you will work the double
decrease in the RS A row or in the RS B row.

The double-knit border of the pillow yields a double-faced tube that has more body than borders consisting of a single thickness of fabric.

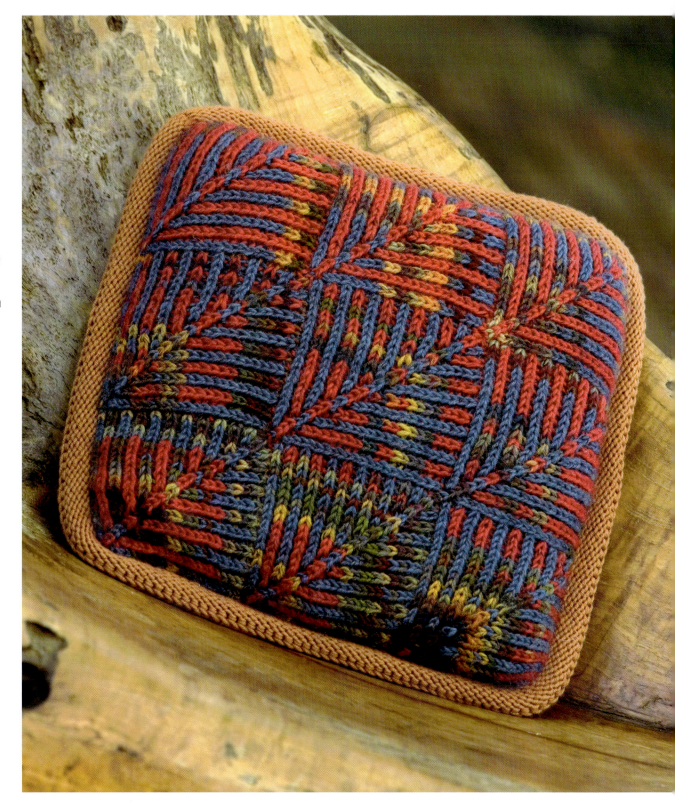

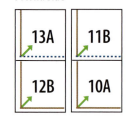

→ Direction of work
— Cast on
---- pick up and knit

1-yarn K1b Mitered Square OVER A MULTIPLE OF 4 STITCHES
Work 8-row repeat of K1b Pattern with decreases as follows:
Row 1 (RS) Slip 1, *k1, k1b; repeat from * until 3 stitches before center, k1, SSK, k1b, **k1, k1b; repeat from **, end k1, turn.
Row 2 (WS) Slip 1, *p1, p1b; repeat from *, until 3 stitches before center, p1, p2tog, **p1, p1b; repeat from **, end p1, turn.
Row 3 (RS) Slip 1, *k1, k1b; repeat from *, end k1, turn.
Row 4 (WS) Slip 1, *p1, p1b; repeat from *, end p1, turn.
Row 5 (RS) Slip 1, *k1, k1b; repeat from * to center, k2tog, **k1, k1b; repeat from **, end k1, turn.
Row 6 (WS) Slip 1, *p1, p1b; repeat from * to center, p1, SSP, **p1, p1b; repeat from **, end p1, turn.
Row 7 (RS) Slip 1, *k1, k1b; repeat from *, end k1, turn.
Row 8 (WS) Slip 1, *p1, p1b; repeat from *, end p1, turn.
End after a row 4 when 6 stitches remain.
RS row Slip 1, k1, k1b, k2tog, end k1, turn.
WS row Slip 1, p1, SSP, p1, turn.
RS row SSK, k2, turn.
WS row P3tog, turn. This last stitch will be the first stitch of the next mitered square.

Second Side
Square 10
With larger circular needle and A and using long-tail loop cast-on, cast on 18 stitches, place marker, cast on 18 stitches. Purl 1 row. With A, work 1-yarn K1b Mitered Square.

Square 11
With last stitch of previous square on needle and B, pick up and knit 17 stitches along top of previous square, place marker; using loop cast-on, cast on 18 stitches, turn. Purl 1 row. Continue as for square 10. Cut yarn, pull tail through last stitch.

Square 12
With B, work as for Square 10.
Square 13
With A, work as for Square 11.

Finishing
Border With C and one circular needle, pick up and knit 48 stitches along each edge of the 9-square side of pillow—192 stitches. Cut yarn. With 2-square pieces arranged as shown above and using C and another needle, pick up and knit 48 stitches along each outside edge of 4-square side of the pillow.
Joining round With WS of pillow pieces together and using smaller needle, slip 1 from back needle, k1 from front needle—384 stitches.
Round 1 *P1, sl1 wyif; repeat from *.
Round 2 *Sl1 wyib, k1; repeat from *. Work these two rounds a total of 4 times. ***Next round*** * SSK; repeat from *—192 stitches. P2tog bind off.
Buttonhole band With RS facing and C, pick up and knit 48 stitches along edge of 2-square piece, turn. Knit 1 row, placing a marker every 6 stitches. Purl 1 row, knit 1 row. ***Next row*** *P2tog bind off to marker; purl-chain 4 chain stitches; repeat from *, end bind off 6. Sew ends of band to border.
Block. Sew on buttons to match chain loops. Insert pillow form.

ORIENTATION TIP When the number of stitches is a multiple of 4, work the decreases of Rows 1 and 2 next. When the number of stitches is a multiple of 4+2, work the decreases of Rows 5 and 6 next.

The stitch-to-row ratio makes k1b stitch patterns perfect candidates for mitered squares: two decrease rows are worked per 8 rows in the Mitered Squares Pillow.

The 2-yarn mitered square is worked over an odd number of stitches with a centered double decrease. The 1-yarn mitered square is worked over an even number of stitches with two paired decreases, giving the knitter two variants of the mitered square technique.

The button band integrates button loops into the bind-off using a 'knit-chain' technique.

Child & Baby

94

100

The **Check It Out Booties** in mix-and-match colors bounce horizontal lines off vertical lines, and are all tied up in contrasting colors.

Railroad Tracks with its fine gauge, intricate stitch pattern, and sophisticated colors is a chic sweater, putting it a notch above a plain and simple kid's garment.

92

The dazzling array of shades in the **Blocks of Color Blanket** will brighten things up.

Column Pattern

☐ K on RS, p on WS
▽ K1b on RS, p1b on WS
▽ Sl 1 wyif on WS

Blocks of Color Blanket

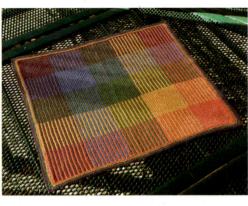

INTERMEDIATE

ONE SIZE
30" x 34"

10cm/4"

38
12
• over Column Pattern

1 2 3 **4** 5 6

Medium weight
A–E • 200 yds each

4.5mm/US 7, or size to obtain gauge, 60cm (24") or longer Longer circular needle of same size for border

&

Stitch markers

3 balls each MISSION FALLS 1824 Cotton in Coral 201 (Color 1), Goldenrod 205 (Color 2), Fennel 301 (Color 3), Sky 403 (Color 4), Phlox 405 (Color 5)

Notes

1 See *Techniques*, page 138, for long-tail loop cast-on, k1b, p1b, intarsia, KOK increase, p2tog bind-off, and slide. *2* At color change on intarsia rows, pick up new A color from under the old A color. *3* Label 1 ball of each color A and another B. Note that solid-colored squares (outlined in red on Color Chart) are worked with balls A and B of the same color. *4* For a larger blanket, work more squares (and more colors) or increase the number of stitches (and rows) in each square by a multiple of 2 stitches and 4 rows.

Blanket

With B1 and using long-tail loop cast-on, cast on 102 stitches. Purl 1 row.
Work in Column Pattern as follows: Intarsia Row 1 (RS) With A1, sl 1, *[k1b, k1] 10 times, place marker (pm); repeat from * with A2, A3, A4, and A5; k1, slide.
Row 2 (RS) With B1, sl 1, *k1, k1b; repeat from *, end k1, turn.
Intarsia Row 3 (WS) With A5, sl 1, *[p1, p1b] to marker, slip marker (sm); repeat from * with A4, A3, A2, and A1; p1, slide.
Row 4 (WS) With B1, sl 1, *p1b, p1; repeat from *, end p1, turn.
Repeat Rows 1–4 fourteen times (or until block is square).
Continue, following Color Chart and changing to B2 for next 56 rows, then B3, B4, and B5. Do not bind off.

Border
With RS facing, Color 1, and longer circular needle, work across top of blanket in pattern; pick up and knit 2 stitches for every 6 rows (2 stitches for 3 Vs) along left edge of blanket; knit into the V at the bottom of each column across cast-on edge; pick up and knit 2 stitches for every 3 Vs along right edge; join. Mark first and last stitches of top and bottom for corners. Purl 1 round. With Color 2, knit 1 round, working KOK increases in marked corner stitches—8 stitches increased; purl 1 round. Repeat last 2 rounds with Color 3 and Color 4. With Color 5, knit 1 round. Bind off using p2tog bind-off.
Sew in ends.

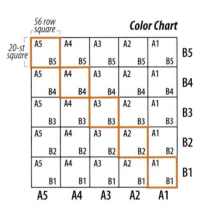

Color Chart

56 row square

20-st square

A5	A4	A3	A2	A1	
B5	B5	B5	B5	B5	**B5**
A5	A4	A3	A2	A1	
B4	B4	B4	B4	B4	**B4**
A5	A4	A3	A2	A1	
B3	B3	B3	B3	B3	**B3**
A5	A4	A3	A2	A1	
B2	B2	B2	B2	B2	**B2**
A5	A4	A3	A2	A1	
B1	B1	B1	B1	B1	**B1**

A5   **A4**   **A3**   **A2**   **A1**

Chart Note
The B colors are worked across all stitches of the row, changing every 56 rows; the A colors change every 20 stitches across each row.

A systematic color study or a free-swinging color-fest? Either way, cuddle up in style in the Blocks of Color Blanket.

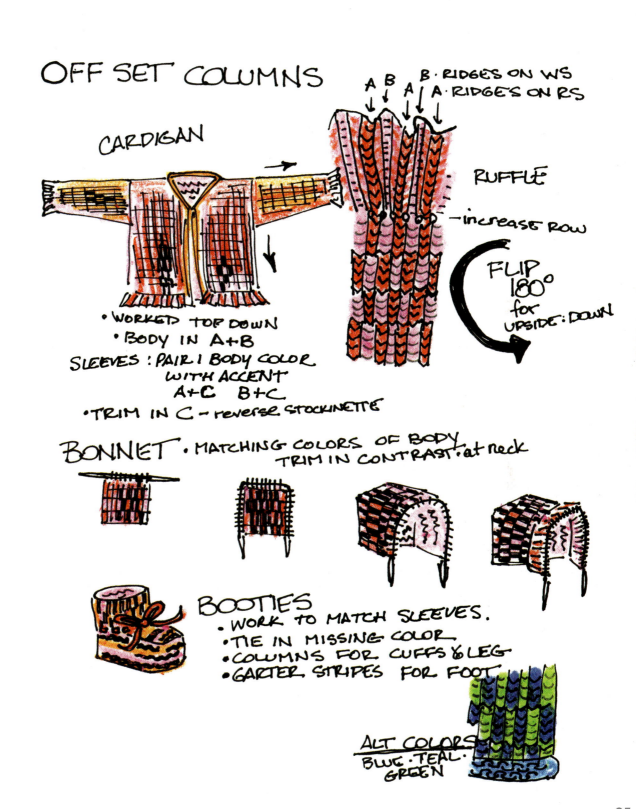

OFF SET COLUMNS

CARDIGAN

A   B   A   B · RIDGES ON WS
              A · RIDGES ON RS

RUFFLE

- increase row

FLIP 180° for UPSIDE·DOWN

- WORKED TOP DOWN
- BODY IN A+B
SLEEVES : PAIR 1 BODY COLOR
        WITH ACCENT
        A+C B+C
- TRIM IN C - reverse STOCKINETTE

BONNET · MATCHING COLORS OF BODY
          TRIM IN CONTRAST · at neck

BOOTIES
- WORK TO MATCH SLEEVES.
- TIE IN MISSING COLOR.
- COLUMNS FOR CUFFS & LEG
- GARTER STRIPES FOR FOOT

ALT COLORS
BLUE · TEAL · GREEN

Jacket Column Pattern OVER AN ODD NUMBER OF STITCHES
Row 1 (RS) With A, k1, *k1b, k1; repeat from * across, slide.
Row 2 (RS) With B, k1, *k1, k1b; repeat from * end k2, turn.
Row 3 (WS) With A, p1, *p1b, p1; repeat from * across, slide.
Row 4 (WS) With B, p1, *p1, p1b; repeat from * end p2, turn.
Repeat rows 1–4 for Column Pattern.

Jacket Column Pattern

2-st repeat

☐ *K on RS, p on WS*
▨ *P on RS, k on WS*
↓ *K1b on RS, p1b on WS*

INTERMEDIATE

STANDARD FIT

6 (12, 18, 24) months
A 20 (21½, 23, 24½)"
B 9 (10, 11, 12)"
C 11½ (12½, 14, 15½)"

Bonnet & Booties
0–6 (6–12) months

10cm/4"
64
22
• *over Column Pattern*

1 **2** 3 4 5 6
Light weight
Red & Pink • 225 (275, 325, 400)
yds each
Orange • 150 (180, 220, 260) yds

2.25mm/US2, or size needed to
obtain gauge, 40cm (16")

2.25mm/US2

2 • 13mm (½")

Stitch holders, stitch markers,
yarn needle

12 MONTHS: 2 balls each DALE OF
NORWAY Baby Ull in color 4018 Red
and 4516 Pink and 1 ball in color
2817 Orange
0-6 Months (blue booties): KOIGU
Painter's Palette Premium Merino
(KPPPM) in color 2232-2

Check It Out Baby

Notes
1 See *Techniques*, page 138, for long-tail loop cast-on, double loop cast-on, k1b, p1b, double increase, p2tog, SSP, 3-needle YO bind-off, graft, button loop, and slide. *2* The cardigan is knit from the top down; the sleeves are picked up along the armhole and knit down to the cuff. *3* For bonnet and booties, if only 1 number is given, it applies to both sizes.

JACKET
Back
Color Sequence *Work 8 rows with Red as A and Pink as B; work 8 rows with Pink as A and Red as B; repeat from*. With Red and using long-tail loop cast-on, cast on 55 (59, 63, 67) stitches. Join Pink at tail-end of needle and purl across row (both yarns are now at same end of needle), turn. Work Column Pattern in Color Sequence until piece measures 4 (4½, 4¾, 5¼)", place marker for sleeve placement. Work until piece measures 8 (9, 10, 11)", end one row before the end of an 8-row color section (a WS A row).
Next row (WS) SSP at beginning and p2tog at end—53 (57, 61, 65) stitches. Put stitches on hold.

Left Front
Cast on 17 (19, 21, 23) stitches and work ½" as for back, end with row 8 of pattern. Work double increase along neck edge next row and every 8 rows (rows 9 and 1 of pattern) 5 times as follows: k1, double increase, work to end of row—27 (29, 31, 33) stitches. Complete as for back— 25 (27, 29, 31) stitches. Put stitches on hold.

Right Front
Work as for left front EXCEPT double increase in next to last stitch of row.
Join shoulders With Red and RS facing and working each piece separately, pick up and knit 1 stitch in each column across top of back and left and right shoulders. With WS held together, work 3-needle YO bind-off to join the 17 (19, 21, 23) stitches of right shoulder. Continue across back of neck with YO bind-off until 17 (19, 21, 23) stitches remain. Join left shoulder with 3-needle YO bind-off.

Left Sleeve
Color sequence *Work 8 rows with Orange as A and Red as B; work 8 rows with Red as A and Orange as B; repeat from*.
With RS facing and Orange, pick up and knit 45 (49, 53, 57) stitches between the markers on left front and back for sleeves, slide. With RS facing and Red, knit 1 row. Beginning with row 3, work Column Pattern until sleeve

Ruffle Pattern 1 OVER AN ODD NUMBER OF STITCHES

Row 1 (RS) With A, k2, *k1b, k3; repeat from *, end k1b, k2, slide.
Row 2 (RS) With B, p2, *p2, p1b, p1; repeat from *, end p3, turn.
Row 3 (WS) With A, p2, p1b *p3, p1b; repeat from *, end p2, slide.
Row 4 (WS) With B, k3, *k1, k1b, k2; repeat from *, end k2, turn.
Repeat rows 1–4 for Ruffle Pattern 1.

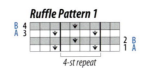

Ruffle Pattern 2 OVER AN EVEN NUMBER OF STITCHES

Round 1 With A, *k3, k1b; repeat from *.
Round 2 With B, *p1, p1b, p2; repeat from *.
Repeat rounds 1–2 for Ruffle Pattern 2.

Ruffle Pattern 2

The simple closure allows the jacket to swing open in an A-line for a baby, but additional loops and buttons on the band could make a more fitted jacket for an older child.

measures approximately 6½ (7½, 8½, 9½)", end one row before the end of an 8-row color section; AT SAME TIME, k2tog at the beginning and SSK at the end every 12 rows 8 (9, 10, 11) times—29 (31, 33, 35) stitches. **Next row** SSP, work to last 2 stitches, p2tog—27 (29, 31, 33) stitches. Put stitches on hold.

Right Sleeve

Color sequence *Work 8 rows with Pink as A and Orange as B; work 8 rows with Orange as A and Pink as B; repeat from*.
Work as for Left Sleeve, picking up and knitting between makers on right front and back in Pink, then knitting 1 row in Orange.

Finishing

Join sleeve and body seams With RS facing, circular needle, and contrasting color (the color not used for this piece), pick up and knit 3 stitches for every 4 Vs along both sides of the sleeve. With WS together work 3-needle YO bind-off to join. Repeat for side seams of body.

Front body and back neck bands With RS facing and contrast color (the color not used for the body), pick up and knit 1 stitch for each V along right front, 1 stitch per column plus 5 extra stitches evenly distributed across back of neck, 1 stitch for each V along the left front. Turn. Knit 1 row, [purl 1 row, knit 1 row] 2 times. Sew live stitches to inside, enclosing the selvedge stitches.

Body ruffle

With RS facing and circular needle only (no yarn), pick up 1 stitch from base of left front edging, place 25 (27, 29, 31) stitches of left front back on needle, pick up 1 stitch from side seam, place 53 (57, 61, 65) stitches of back on needle, pick up 1 stitch from side seam, place 25 (27, 29, 31) stitches of right front on needle, and pick up 1 stitch from base of right front edging—107 (115, 123, 131) stitches. Slide.
Note Work with the same colors for A and B as used in last 8-row section of body.
Increase row (RS) With A, *k1, yo, k1b, yo; repeat from *, end k1, slide. *Next row* With B, purl, turn.
Begin Ruffle Pattern 1 with row 3 and work for approximately 1", end with a RS A row, turn. With A and using YO bind-off, bind off.

Sleeve ruffle

Note Color A is sleeve color A, B is sleeve color B.
With RS facing, A, and dpns, knit 27 (29, 31, 33) sleeve stitches, plus 1 at base of 3-needle bind-off—28 (30, 32, 34) stitches. Join.
Increase round With A, *yo, k1, yo, k1b; repeat from *.
Next round With B, purl.
Work Ruffle Pattern 2 for 1", end with an A round. With WS facing, A, and using YO bind-off, bind off.
Make button loop at base of V-neck. Sew on buttons.

Bonnet and Booties

BONNET

Color sequence *Work 8 rows with Red as A, Pink as B; work 8 rows with Pink as A and Red as B; repeat from *.

Back panel With Red and using long-tail loop cast-on, cast on 15 (17) stitches. Join Pink at tail-end of needle and purl across row (both yarns are now at same end of needle), turn. Work Bonnet Column Pattern in Color Sequence for 44 (48) rows, cut both yarns.

Sides and top With RS facing, dpns, A and starting at lower right corner (where the yarn tails are not hanging), pick up and knit 16 (18) stitches along right side of panel, work 15 (17) stitches in pattern across top, pick up and knit 16 (18) stitches along left side—47 (53) stitches, slide. Tie B onto A tail. With B, k16 (18), work 15 (17) stitches in pattern, k16 (18), turn. Work rows 3 and 4 of the pattern across all stitches. Work 44 (48) rows. Do not cut yarns. Work ruffle as for bottom of jacket over 47 (53) stitches.

Ties With Orange and using long-tail loop cast-on, cast on 70 stitches, turn. P2tog bind off until 1 stitch remains, pull ball of yarn through last loop but do not cut yarn.

With RS facing, pick up and knit along the neck edge of the bonnet: 20 (24) stitches along side panel, 13 (15) along back panel, and 20 (24) along other side panel—53 (63) stitches. Continue, casting on 70 stitches; work p2tog bind-off as for first tie.

Band Work 5 rows reverse stockinette stitch (purl on RS, knit on WS) over the 53 (63) stitches. Sew live stitches to inside, enclosing the edge. Sew in the yarn ends.

BOOTIES

Color sequences: Left Bootie *Work 8 rounds with Orange as A, Red as B; 8 rounds with Red as A, Orange as B; repeat from *.

Right Bootie *Work 8 rounds with Pink as A, Orange as B; 8 rounds with Orange as A, Pink as B; repeat from *.

With B and using double loop cast-on, cast on 20 (24). Join A at non-tail end of needle and purl one row. Divide evenly over 3 or 4 dpns. Place marker for beginning of round. Join, being careful not to twist stitches (purl bumps will be on the outside, forming a decorative ridge). With a single strand of B, knit 1 round.

Leg Work 24 (32) rounds in Bootie Column Pattern. With A, purl 1 round.

Eyelet round Yo, k1, yo, k2tog, yo, k1] 5 (6) times —30 (36) stitches. With B, knit 1 round, purl 1 round.

Front flap Work back and forth on the first 12 (14) stitches. *With A, knit 2 rows; with B, knit 2 rows; repeat from * 5 (6) times—12 (14) garter ridges. Cut yarns.

Foot Distribute remaining stitches over 2 dpn, placing marker in the center. Joining yarns and adding dpns as needed, work in the round as follows: With A, k9 (11), pick up and k12 (14) along side of flap, k12 (14) across front of flap, pick up and k12 (14) along other side of flap, k9 (11)—54 (64) stitches. With A, p20 (24), p2tog, p 5 (6), place marker, p5 (6), p2tog (stitch before and after marker), p20 (24)—52 (62) stitches. **With B, knit 1 round, purl 1 round. With A, knit 1 round, purl 1 round. Repeat from ** a total of—6 garter ridges.

Sole [Decrease round K2tog, knit to 2 stitches before marker, SSK, k2tog, knit to 2 stitches before marker, SSK—4 stitches decreased. Purl 1 round.] with A, B, A, B—36 (46) stitches. With A, knit 18 (23) stitches on another needle, graft the bottom of the sole.

Ties With contrast yarn and using long-tail loop cast-on, cast on 100 stitches. Using p2tog bind-off, bind off until 1 stitch remains, pull ball of yarn through last loop and cut yarn. Knot ends tightly and cut close to the knot. Thread through eyelets. Sew in the yarn ends.

Bonnet Column Pattern

Row 1 (RS) With A, k1, *k1, k1b; repeat from *, end k2, slide.
Row 2 (RS) With B, k1, *k1b, k1; repeat from *, turn.
Row 3 (WS) With A, p1, *p1, p1b; repeat from *, end p2, slide.
Row 4 (WS) With B, p1, *p1b, p1; repeat from *, turn.
Repeat rows 1—4 for Bonnet Column Pattern.

Bonnet Column Pattern

2-st repeat

Bootie Column Pattern OVER AN EVEN NUMBER OF STITCHES

Round 1 (RS) With A, *k1, k1b; repeat from *.
Round 2 (RS) With B, *k1b, k1; repeat from *.
Repeat rounds 1—2 for Bootie Column Pattern.

☐ K on RS, p on WS
☑ K1b on RS, p1b on WS

Bootie Pattern

2-st repeat

The 4-strand braid shown on page 143 of the Technique Section makes great ties for the Bonnet and Booties.

K1b and Kids

KID KNITS : Simplicity & Quality
1. Simple shapes
2. Fine weight yarn
3. Elegant jewel tones are ageless.
4. Special buttons for closure
5. Bright border finishes as a zinger.
6. Easy care / natural blend fibers.

PULLOVER WITH NO SHOULDER SEAMS
BOAT NECK FOR EASY DRESSING
mother of pearl buttons in 4 jewel colors.

garter ridges
stabilize fabric
widthwise

jewel colors

C
A
B & C
A
B
A & C
B
C
A & B (8 rows Pattern)
C
B
A — contrast for trim & seams.

Broken Column Pattern OVER AN ODD NUMBER OF STITCHES

Note For rows 1–12, A is Purple, B is Green, and C is Blue.

Row 1 (RS) With A, knit; slide.

Row 2 (RS) With B, k1, *k1, k1b; repeat from *, end k2, turn. Tie ends.

Row 3 (WS) With A, p1, *p1b, p1; repeat from *, slide.

Row 4 (WS) With B, p1, *p1, p1b; repeat from *, end p2, turn.

Railroad Tracks

Notes

1 See *Techniques*, page 138, for long-tail loop cast-on, k1b, p1b, slide, Make 1, k2tog, YO, overhand knot, p2tog bind-off, and 3-needle YO bind-off. **2** Do not join yarn in the middle of a row. **3** Do not weave in ends; leave 6" tails and tie ends together in overhand knot as specified in pattern.

Back

With Red and using long-tail loop cast-on, cast on 75 (87, 99, 111) stitches.

Lower band Knit 1 row. Cut Red; tie ends. ***Row 1*** (RS) With Purple, knit. ***Row 2*** (WS) Knit, cut yarn, tie ends.

Rows 3–4 With Green, repeat rows 1 and 2. ***Rows 5–6*** With Blue, repeat rows 1 and 2.

Work in Broken Column Pattern until piece measures 8½ (9½, 10½, 11½)", place underarm markers. Continue in pattern until work measures 14 (15½, 17, 18½)", end after any 12-row color grouping (row 12, 24 or 36 of stitch pattern). ******

Upper band With color not used in last 4 rows, knit 2 rows. With Red, knit 1 row. Bind off using p2tog bind-off.

Front

Work as for back to******.

Buttonhole band With color not used in last 4 rows, *k 5 (6, 7, 8), k2tog, yo; repeat from * once, knit 45 (53, 61, 69), k2tog, yo, k 5 (6, 7, 8), k2tog, yo, k 7 (8, 9, 10), turn. Knit one row. With Red, knit 1 row and bind off as for back.

Sleeves

Cast on 39 (41, 43, 45) stitches and work lower band as for back.

Work in Broken Column Pattern, increasing as follows: ***Increase row*** (RS) Make 1 after first stitch and before last stitch every 8 rows 7 (8, 9, 10) times, every 10 rows 7 (8, 9, 10) times—67 (73, 79, 85) stitches. Work even until sleeve measures 10 (11, 12, 13)", end after a 12-row color grouping. At end of first sleeve, place stitches on hold. Leave second sleeve on needle.

Finishing

Work all pick-ups and joins with RS facing and Red.

Join sleeves and body Knit 1 row across top of sleeve. With upper bands of front overlapping back and extra needle, pick up 67 (73, 79, 85) stitches along armhole between underarm markers. With body facing, join sleeve to body pieces with 3-needle YO bind-off. Repeat with second sleeve on other side of body.

INTERMEDIATE

STANDARD FIT

Child's 2–4 (6–8, 10–12, 14–16)

A 25 (29, 33, 37)"

B 14 (15½, 17, 18½)"

C 16¼ (18¼, 20¼, 22¼)"

10cm/4"

64

24

• over Broken Column Pattern

1 **2** 3 4 5 6

Fine weight

Purple, Green, Blue • 325 (400, 475, 575) yds each

Red • 70 (90, 110, 130) yds

3.25mm/US 3, or size to obtain gauge, 60cm (24") or longer

Extra needle for 3-needle bind-off

4 • 15mm (½")

Stitch holders and yarn needle

Child's 2–4 2 skeins each BROWN SHEEP Cotton Fine, in colors CF-710 Prosperous Plum (Purple), CF-400 New Age Teal (Green), and CF-760 Emperor's Robe (Blue); 1 skein CF-930 Candy Apple (Red)

Row 5 (RS) With A, k1, *k1b, k1; repeat from *, slide.

Row 6 (RS) With B, k1, *k1, k1b; repeat from *, end k2, turn.

Row 7 (WS) With A, p1, *p1b, p1; repeat from *, slide. Cut yarn.

Row 8 (WS) With B, p1, *p1, p1b; repeat from *, end p2, turn. Cut yarn; tie ends.

Row 9 (RS) With C, k1, *k1b, k1; repeat from *.

Row 10 (WS) With C, knit; turn. Cut yarn, tie ends.

Row 11 (RS) With B, knit; turn.

Row 12 (WS) With B, knit; turn. Cut yarn, tie ends.

Rows 13–24 Repeat rows 1–12, EXCEPT A is Blue, B is Purple, and C is Green.

Rows 25–36 Repeat rows 1–12, EXCEPT A is Green, B is Blue, and C is Purple.

Repeat Rows 1–36 for Broken Column Pattern.

- Purple
- Green
- Blue

☐ K on RS, p on WS
⊟ K on WS
⬇ K1b on RS, p1b on WS
— cut yarns; tie ends

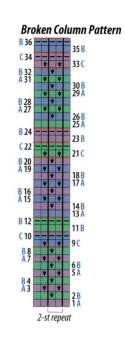

Broken Column Pattern

2-st repeat

Side and sleeve seam Pick up and knit 2 stitches for every 3 Vs along left front/sleeve edges. With extra needle, pick up and knit along left back/sleeve. Join with 3-needle YO bind-off, working from hem to cuff. Repeat for right front/sleeve and right back/sleeve.

Tie overhand knots in any remaining yarn tails on WS. Sew in any visible tails near cuff and bottom edges. Trim ends to approximately ½".

Sew buttons on back band.

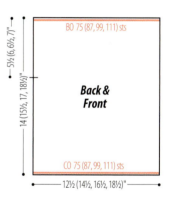

BO 75 (87, 99, 111) sts

Back & Front

CO 75 (87, 99, 111) sts

5½ (6, 6½, 7)"

14 (15½, 17, 18½)"

12½ (14½, 16½, 18½)"

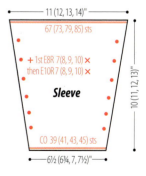

11 (12, 13, 14)"

67 (73, 79, 85) sts

+ 1st E8R 7 (8, 9, 10) ✕
then E10R 7 (8, 9, 10) ✕

Sleeve

CO 39 (41, 43, 45) sts

10 (11, 12, 13)"

6½ (6¾, 7, 7½)"

With its combination of the Column Pattern and garter stitch, Railroad Tracks will chug its way right into your kid's heart.

106
Bottoms Up! — The crowning glory of columns of color.

118

Weaving a luxurious, silky yarn over the colorful base of the **Tattersall Scarf** will transform your columns into plaids.

129

You'll have toasty tootsies in these **Pinwheel Socks**! Legs and feet in the Column Pattern, paired with garter stitch for heels and toes.

HeadToToe

Column Pattern OVER AN EVEN NUMBER OF STITCHES
Round 1 (RS) With A, *k1, k1b; repeat from * .
Round 2 (RS) With B, *k1b, k1; repeat from * .

Column Pattern

2-st repeat

EASY+

Approximately 12" across
and 10" high

10cm/4"

22

8

• **Over Column Pattern
before felting**

1 2 3 **4** 5 6

Medium weight
A • 190 yds
B1 • 100 yds
B2 • 110 yds

8mm/US 11, or size to obtain
gauge, 60cm (24") long
Second needle for welt

Five 8mm/US 11

&

Yarn needle and stitch markers

*1 skein each BROWN SHEEP Lamb's
Pride Worsted in color M-06, Deep
Charcoal (A) and color M-75, Blue
Heirloom (B1) and 1 skein NORO
Kureyon in color 52 (B2)*

Bottoms Up!

Notes

1 See *Techniques*, page 138, for long-tail loop cast-on, k1b, I-cord, k2tog, SSK, double increase, kf&b, yo, 3-needle bind-off, YO bind-off, working with dpn, and felting. **2** The double increase is always worked after you have worked a k1. **3** Work change from color A to color B at beginning of round; work loosely and do not twist the yarns. **4** Change from dpn to circular needles when there are enough stitches.

BAG

Base

With A and using long-tail loop cast-on, cast on 8 stitches. Join B1 at tail-end of needle and knit across row (A and B1 are now at same end of needle). Distribute on 4 dpn. Join and mark beginning of round. Using A and B1, work 2 rounds in Column Pattern. **Increase round** With A, [work to last stitch on dpn, double increase] 4 times—8 stitches increased. Continue in pattern, working increase round every other A round for a total of 8 increase rounds—72 stitches. AT SAME TIME, when there are enough stitches, change to circular needle, placing a marker between each dpn's stitches; work double increase in stitch before marker. Work 2 rounds in pattern. With A, purl 6 rounds.

Make welt Using second circular needle, pick up B stitches 6 rounds earlier (in the round where B is visible for the last time); knit them together with A stitches on the needle. End B1. With A, knit 1 round.

Body of bag

Work Column Pattern using B2 until it is used up, end with a B round.

Eyelets

Round 1 With A, [k3, k2tog, SSK, k2] 8 times. **Round 2** [P4, yo, p3] 8 times. **Round 3** [K4, k1 and p1 into yo of previous row, k3] 8 times. Purl 1 round, knit 1 round, purl 1 round. Make welt, skipping the 2 eyelet stitches so holes remain open. With B1, [knit 1 round, purl 1 round] 3 times.

Make welt and bind off Using second circular needle, pick up A stitches 6 rounds earlier; work 3-needle bind-off with B1 stitches on the main needle. Sew in yarn ends.

Straps

Make two, one A and one B1. Cast on 4 stitches and work 48" length of I-cord. Holding straps together, weave them through the holes. Sew the ends of each together to form a loop. Felt bag in washing machine.

Base Shaping

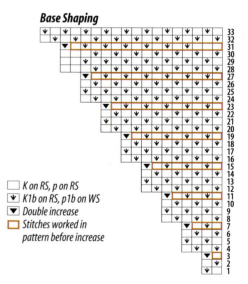

☐ K on RS, p on RS
⊡ K1b on RS, p1b on WS
▼ Double increase
☐ Stitches worked in pattern before increase

Bottoms up — the right way
to carry your felted bag to
show off the swirled pattern.

1 skein each color as follows:
Tall Pillbox: BROWN SHEEP Lamb's Pride Worsted in color M-07 Sable (A) and NORO Kureyon in color 178 (B)
Short Pillbox: Lamb's Pride Worsted in color M-06 Deep Charcoal (A) and color M-81 Red Baron (B)
Hat with Garter Brim: Lamb's Pride Worsted in M-185 Aubergine (A)) and NORO Kureyon color 90 (B)
Hat with 7-section Brim: Lamb's Pride Worsted in color M-05 Onyx (A) and NORO Kureyon color 40 (B)

PILLBOX

4-section Crown
Work as for Bag Base EXCEPT use B instead of B1 and work a total of 7 increase rows—64 stitches.
Hat
Work in Column Pattern for 45 rounds for the shorter pillbox or 55 rounds for the taller pillbox, ending after an A round (round 1 of pattern). Work welt. Bind off very loosely. Felt.

HAT WITH GARTER BRIM

Work as for Bag Base EXCEPT work increase rounds as follows:
First increase round With A, *work 1, double increase; repeat from * around—8 stitches increased. ***Second increase round*** Work 3 stitches before double increase. Continue to work 2 more stitches in pattern before double increase on each increase round for a total of 6 increase rounds—56 stitches. Leave beginning of round marker, remove others. Work 12" in Column Pattern, end with B round (round 2 of pattern).
Brim
Increase round 1 With A, *k1, kf&b; repeat from *—84 stitches. Purl 1 round. With B, knit 1 round, purl 1 round. ***Increase round 2*** With A, *k14, kf&b, place marker; repeat from *—90 stitches. Purl 1 round. With B, knit 1 round, purl 1 round. ***Next increase round*** *Work to 1 stitch before marker, kf&b; repeat from *—6 stitches increased. Purl 1 round. With B, knit 1 round, purl 1 round. Repeat last 4 rounds 5 more times—120 stitches. End A. With B and using YO bind-off, bind off. Thread cast-on tail through cast-on loops and pull tight. Fasten ends. Felt.

HAT WITH 7-SECTION BRIM

4-section Crown
Work as for Garter-brimmed hat.
Brim
Work 2 rounds Column Pattern, placing a marker every 8 stitches. ***Increase round*** With A, *k1, double increase, work to next marker; repeat from*—14 stitches increased.
Continue to work Increase round every other A round a total of 4 times—112 stitches. Work 2 rounds Column Pattern. With B, knit 1 round, purl 1 round, and bind off, using YO bind-off. Sew in ends. Felt.

HAT WITH 3-SECTION BRIM

3-section Crown
With A and using long-tail loop cast-on, cast on 6 stitches. Join B at tail-end of needle and knit across row (A and B are now at same end of needle). Distribute stitches on 3 dpn (2 stitches on each) and mark beginning of round. Work 2 rounds in Column Pattern.
Increase round With A, *k1, double increase, work to next dpn; repeat from*—6 stitches increased. Continue in pattern, working Increase round every other A round for a total of 9 increase rounds—60 stitches. AT SAME TIME when there are enough stitches, change to circular needle, placing a marker between each dpn's stitches. Work 32 rounds even, end with A round. Do not cut B.
Garter band
With A, [purl 1 round, knit 1 round] 3 times.
Brim
Work 2 rounds Column Pattern. ***Increase round*** With A, *k1, double increase, work to next marker; repeat from*—6 stitches increased. Continue in pattern, working Increase round every other A round for a total of 5 increase rounds—90 stitches. Work 3 rounds even. With A knit 1 round, purl 1 round. Bind off using YO bind-off. Fasten ends. Felt.

The garter band provides an attractive accent and also has a function: it gives the hat a nice snug fit.

A Rubbermaid size 10 bowl tends to be a good hat mold. For a smaller fit, pull the hat part way over the bowl; for a larger hat, pull it further down the slanted sides of the bowl.

Tall Pillbox

Hat with 3-section Brim…

…and 3-section Crown

Hat with Garter Brim

Short Pillbox

Hat with 7-section Brim

109

Fringed Column Pattern OVER AN EVEN NUMBER OF STITCHES
Note Leave a 6" tail at beginning and end of each row for fringe.
Odd-numbered rows (RS) K1, *k1, k1b; repeat from *, end k1, cut yarn, slide.
Even-numbered rows (RS) K1, *k1b, k1; repeat from *, end k1, cut yarn, slide.
Color Sequence change color for each row as follows: *[A, B] 2×; [C, D] 2×; [E, A] 2×, [B, C] 2×; [D, E] 2×; repeat from *

Fringed Garter Pattern
Note Leave a tail of 6" at beginning and end of each row for fringe.
All rows Knit, cut yarn, turn.
Color Sequence Change color every other row as follows: A, C, E, B, D.

Fringed Column Pattern
2-st repeat

A Family Affair

Notes
1 See *Techniques*, page 138, for long-tail loop cast-on, overhand knot, k1b, p1b, slide, k2tog, double decrease, knit loop bind-off, and fringe. *2* When you work scarf, turn work at end of each garter row so that you are always working a knit row, and slide the stitches at the end of each column row so you are always working with RS facing. *3* For cap, change to double-pointed needles (dpn) when necessary. *4* For cap and mittens, do not cut yarns when you change colors. Carry the yarns on the inside. In Garter Stitch, twist as you change colors: lay yarns not being used to the left and bring up the color you need on the right. In Column Pattern, do not twist: leave yarns not being used to the right and bring up the color you need on the left.

Scarf
With larger needle and A and using long-tail loop cast-on, cast on 120 (160, 180) stitches. Cut yarn leaving a 6" tail, turn. *Work 10 rows Fringed Garter Stitch beginning Color Sequence with second A row, end with a RS A row. Work 20 rows Fringed Column Pattern beginning with Row 2 of Color Sequence and ending with Row 1. Repeat from * 1 (2, 2) more times, then work 8 rows of Fringed Garter Stitch beginning with second row of A, end with D but do not cut yarn, turn. With WS facing, continue with D and bind off with knit loop bind-off. Tighten edge stitches as you tie pairs of ends together with an overhand knot.

Cap
With smaller circular needle and E and using long-tail loop cast-on, cast on 60 (66, 72) stitches, turn. Purl 1 row. Join, mark beginning of round. Knit 1 round. *Next round* *K1b, k1; repeat from *. Work 24 (32, 32) rounds in Column Pattern (see page 112) following Color Sequence.
Garter Band
Round 1 With A, *k1, k1b; repeat from *. *Round 2* With A, purl. Work 16 (20, 24) rounds in Fringed Garter Pattern following Color Sequence. Turn work inside out, take all of the yarns to the back (WS will become RS; see photo, page 112). Work 28 (36, 40) rounds in Column Pattern.
Crown
Place marker every 10 (11, 12) stitches—6 sections. *Round 1* With A, *k1, k1b; repeat from *. With A, purl 1 round.
Decrease Round With C, *knit to 2 sts before the marker, k2tog—6 stitches decreased. With C, purl 1 round. [Work Decrease round. Purl 1 round] with E, B, and D. Repeat last 2 rounds following Garter Color Sequence until 6 stitches remain. Cut yarns and thread tail of last color through remaining stitches. Pull tightly and secure.

The colors in the columns and in the garter stitch are arranged from dark-to-light or in rainbow sequence (for the kids' set). Just build these sequences and read your knitting as you go.

INTERMEDIATE +

Child's (Woman's, Man's)
Scarves 34 x 5½ (48 x 8½, 51 x 8½)" without fringe
Caps 18 (20, 22)" circumference
Mittens 6½ (7½, 8½)"

10cm/4"
48/56/56
14/16/16
• over garter stitch

1 2 **3** 4 5 6
Light weight
A–E • 75 (125, 150) yds each

Scarf 4mm/US 6, or size to obtain gauge, 60cm (24") or longer
Cap 3.5mm/US 4, or size to obtain gauge, 40cm (16")

Cap & Mittens 3.5mm/US 4, or size to obtain gauge

Markers

Man's Set: 2 balls each in DALE OF NORWAY Hauk in color 0083 Charcoal (A), 2931 Beige (B), 0007 Medium Gray (C), 0020 White (D), 0004 Light Gray (E)
Woman's Set: 2 balls each in DALE OF NORWAY Hauk in color 5563 Navy Blue (A), 5545 Medium Blue (B), 5364 Dark Blue (C), 5943 Light Blue (D), 5646 Royal Blue (E)
Child's Set: 1 ball each in DALE OF NORWAY Hauk in color 4018 red (A), 9155 Green (B), 3418 Orange (C), 5646 Blue (D), 2427 Yellow (E)

Column Pattern OVER AN EVEN NUMBER OF STITCHES
Odd-numbered rounds (RS) *K1, k1b; repeat from *.
Even-numbered rounds (RS) *K1b, k1; repeat from *.
Color Sequence Change color for each row as follows:
*[A, B] 2×; [C, D] 2×; [E, A] 2×; [B, C] 2×; [D, E] 2×; repeat from *.

Column Pattern

2 B
1 A

2-st repeat

☐ Knit
⤓ K1b

Garter Stitch Pattern
Odd-numbered rounds (RS) Knit.
Even-numbered rounds (WS) Purl.
Color Sequence Change color every other row as follows: A, C, E, B, D.

Mittens (make 2)

Cuff

With dpn and A and using long-tail loop cast-on, cast on 24 (28, 32) stitches, turn. Purl 1 row. Distribute stitches on 3 or 4 dpn. Join, mark beginning of round. Work Garter Stitch, beginning Color Sequence with round 3, until you have worked 18 (28, 28) rounds. With D, decrease 2 stitches over next round—22 (26, 30) stitches. Purl 1 round. **Begin Column Pattern Color Sequence** With A, knit 1 round.

Thumb gusset

Increase Round 2 With B, [k1b, k1]; 5 (6, 7) times, double increase, place marker, k1, place marker, double increase, [k1, k1b]; 4 (5, 6) times, k1—26 (30, 34) stitches. Continue with Column Pattern beginning Color Sequence with round 3. **Increase Round 9** With E, work in pattern to **2** stitches before marker, double increase, k1, slip marker, k1b, slip marker, k1, double increase, work to end of round—30 (34, 38) stitches. **Increase Round 16** With C, work in pattern to **3** stitches before marker, double increase, work 2 stitches in pattern, slip marker, k1, slip marker, 2 stitches in pattern, double increase, work to end of round—34 (38, 42) stitches.

For Child's size

Round 17 With D, work in pattern. **Round 18** With E, work to 5 stitches before marker, place next 11 stitches on hold for thumb, loop cast on 1 stitch, work to end of round—24 stitches.

For Woman's and Man's size

Work 6 rounds in pattern. **Increase Round 23** With A, work to **4** stitches before marker, double increase, k1, k1b, k1, slip marker, k1b, slip marker, k1, k1b, k1, double increase, work to end of round—42 (46) stitches. **Round 24** With B, work in pattern. **Round 25** With C, work to 7 stitches before the marker, place the next 15 stitches on hold for thumb, loop cast on 1 stitch, work to end of round—28 (32) stitches.

All sizes

Work even in pattern over 24 (28, 32) stitches until mitten measures 4¼ (6, 7)" above cuff, end with 1 round of A (round 1 or round 10 of the Color Sequence). With A, purl 1 round.

Shape top of hand

Place marker every 6 (7, 8) stitches—4 sections. **Round 1** With C, *knit to 2 stitches before marker, k2tog; repeat from *. **Round 2** With C, purl. Repeat last 2 rows, following Garter Color Sequence until 8 stitches remain. Cut yarns and run tail of last color through remaining stitches. Pull tightly and secure.

Thumb

Return 11 (15, 15) stitches to dpns. Pick up one extra stitch—12 (16, 16) stitches. Join and work around in Column Pattern until thumb measures 1¼ (1½, 2)", end with a single round of a color.

Shape top of thumb

With same color, purl 1 round. **Round 1** With next color in Garter Sequence, [k2tog, k2] 3 (4, 4) times—9 (12, 12) stitches. **Round 2** With that color, purl. **Round 3** With next color, [k2tog, k1] 3 (4, 4) times—6 (8, 8) stitches. **Round 4** With that color, purl. Cut yarns and run tail of last color through remaining stitches. Pull tightly and secure.

These accessories benefit from garter stitch having a slightly smaller gauge than the Column Pattern: the band under the folded-up brim of the hat ensures a snug fit and the tips of the mittens make them durable. The pieces all emphasize the interplay of horizontal stripes with the vertical columns.

Column Pattern OVER AN EVEN NUMBER OF STITCHES
Round 1 and odd-numbered rounds (RS) *K1, k1b; repeat from *.
Round 2 and even-numbered rounds (RS) *K1b, k1; repeat from *.

Ruffle Pattern OVER AN EVEN NUMBER OF STITCHES
Round 1 (RS) With A, *k2, k1b, k1; repeat from *.
Round 2 (RS) With B, *p1b, p3; repeat from *.

Column Pattern

2 B
1 A

2-st repeat

Ruffle Pattern

2 B
1 A

4-st repeat

☐ Knit
▨ Purl
▾ K1b
▾ P1b

Y-shaped increases run straight up the side of the thumb, shaping this unconventional gusset without interrupting the flow of the vertical columns.

Seeing Doubles

Notes
1 See *Techniques*, page 138, for long-tail loop cast-on, k1b, p1b, double increase, p2tog bind-off, 4-strand braid, and working on dpns. *2* When you change from yarn A to yarn B at beginning of round, work loosely and do not twist the yarns. *3* For cap, change to circular needle if desired. *4* Reverse A and B colors on second gauntlet.

Gauntlets (Make 2)
With A and using long-tail loop cast-on, cast on 64 stitches. Join B at tail-end of needle and purl across row (A and B are at same end of needle). Distribute on 4 needles. Join, being careful not to twist stitches. Place marker. Work ruffle pattern for 1½", ending with a B round (round 2 of pattern). **Decrease round** With A, *k1, S2KP2b; repeat from *—32 stitches. Continue in Column Pattern until the gauntlet measures 4", end with a B round. *Thumb gusset: Increase Round 1* With A, work *15* stitches in pattern, double increase, work to end—34 stitches. Work 6 rounds in pattern. *Increase Round 8* With B, work *16* stitches in pattern, double increase, work to end—36 stitches. ***Continue to increase 2 stitches every 7th round as follows: Round 15* Work *17* stitches. *Round 22* Work *18* stitches. *Round 29* Work *19* stitches. *Round 36* Work *20* stitches—44 stitches. *Thumb opening: Round 43* Work 15 stitches, p2tog bind off 13 stitches, work to end—31 stitches. *Next round* Pick up and knit 1 in first and in last bound-off stitch, pass first stitch over second, work to end—32 sts. Work 1½" in pattern, end with a B round. With A, p2tog bind off.

Cap
With A, a double-pointed needle (dpn), and using long-tail loop cast-on, cast on 10 stitches. Join B at tail-end of needle and knit across row (A and B are at same end of needle). Distribute stitches over 4 dpn. Join and mark beginning of round. Work 2 rounds in Column Pattern, placing a marker after each 2-stitch repeat on first round. *Increase Round 1* With A, *work *1* stitch in pattern, double increase; repeat from *—20 stitches. *Rounds 2, 4, and all non-increase, even-numbered rounds* With B, *k1b, k1; repeat from *. *Rounds 3, 5, and all non-increase, odd-numbered rounds* With A, *k1, k1b; repeat from *. *Increase Round 6* With B, *work *2* stitches in pattern, double increase, work in pattern to next marker; repeat from *—30 stitches. ***Continue to increase 10 stitches every 5th round as follows: Round 11* *Work *3* stitches in pattern. *Round 16* *Work *4* stitches. *Round 21,* *Work *5* stitches. *Round 26* *Work *6* stitches. *Round 31* *Work *7* stitches. *Round 36* *Work *8* stitches. *Round 41* *Work *9* stitches. *Round 46* *Work *10* stitches. *Round 51* *Work *11* stitches—120 stitches. Work even in Column Pattern for 3", end with an A round. With A, purl 1 round. [Knit 1 round, purl 1 round] with B, A, B, A, B 2. With A, knit 1 round and bind off using p2tog bind-off. Thread cast-on tail through loops of cast-on and tighten. Make a 4-strand braid and sew it to the garter edging to cover the beginning rounds. Sew in ends.

INTERMEDIATE +

Adult Medium

10cm/4"

64

20

• over Column Pattern
• For convenience, work gauge swatch back and forth, following Column Pattern on page 4.

1 **2** 3 4 5 6

Fine weight
A & B • 200 yds each

Five 2.75mm/US 2, or size to obtain gauge

Optional 2.75mm/US 2, 40cm (16")

&

Stitch markers, yarn needle, and waste yarn

KOIGU Premium Merino 2 skeins each in colors P 910 solid (A) and 1125 multi (B)

S2KP2b

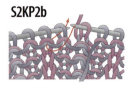

1 With right needle, slip into row below second stitch on left needle, and into first stitch. Slip the stitches together to right needle as if to knit.

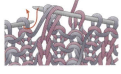

2 Knit next stitch.

3 Pass slipped stitches over knit stitch and off right needle: 3 stitches become 1.

The result is a centered double decrease, continuing your line of color.

Scarf Pattern

All rows Slip 1 purlwise with yarn in front, [p1, p1b] 8 times (to marker) [k1, k1b] 8 times, k1, turn.

Scarf Pattern

Hat pattern:
Round 1 *K1, k1b; repeat from *, end k1.
Round 2 *K1b, k1; repeat from *, end k1b.

Hat Pattern
2-st repeat

K1b Pattern
Round 1 (RS) *K1, k1b; repeat from *.
Round 2 (RS) *K1b, k1; repeat from *.

Column Pattern
2-st repeat

Medium adult
48"x8"

10cm/4"

40/44

13/14
• over K1b Pattern

1 2 3 **4** 5 6

Medium weight
500 yards

3.75mm/US 5, or size to obtain gauge

3.75mm/US 5, 40cm (16") long
Optional: Straight or longer circular needles for scarf

&

Stitch marker

2 skeins MOUNTAIN COLORS Alpaca Blend in color Huckleberry

About Face

Notes
1 See *Techniques*, page 138, for long-tail loop cast-on, k1b, p1b, double increase, p2tog, I-cord, loop cast-on, grafting, and working with dpns. **2** Hat is worked from the top down. **3** Change to circular needle when stitches fit easily around needle. **4** For a hat and scarf set, make the hat first, then use the rest of the yarn for the scarf.

Edging Using loop cast-on, cast 2 stitches onto left needle. **Row 1** (RS) P1, p2tog (edging stitch together with scarf stitch). **Row 2** (WS) P2. Repeat rows 1–2. Bind off last 2 stitches.

SCARF
Leaving a tail of 5 yards and using long-tail loop cast-on, cast on 34 stitches. ***Set-up row*** P17, place marker, k17, turn. Work in Scarf Pattern until 4 yards of yarn remain, or to desired length. Work Edging across all scarf stitches.

With RS facing, slip needle into scarf cast-on loops—34 stitches. Using tail of yarn, work edging. Block scarf.

HAT
With double-pointed needle and using long-tail loop cast-on, cast on 9 stitches. Knit 1 row. Distribute stitches over 3 or 4 dpn. Join, and mark beginning of round. Work 2 rounds in K1b Pattern. ***Increase Round 3*** *K1, double increase; repeat from *, end k1—17 stitches.
Work 3 rounds even in pattern. ***Increase Round 7*** *Work **3** stitches in pattern (k1, k1b, k1), double increase; repeat from *, k1—25 stitches. Work 3 rounds even in pattern. ***Continue to increase 8 stitches every 4th round as follows: Round 11*** *Work **5** stitches—33 stitches. **Round 15** *Work **7** stitches—41 stitches.
Round 19 *Work **9** stitches—49 stitches. **Round 23** *Work **11** stitches—57 stitches.
Round 27 *Work **13** stitches—65 stitches. Work even on 65 stitches until 7½" from cast-on. Knit 6 rounds. Work even in K1b Pattern for 2½". Work edging EXCEPT don't bind off last 2 stitches, graft them to 2 cast-on stitches. Fasten ends. Thread cast-on tail through loops at beginning of hat and pull to close center. Block hat.
Optional trim
Knit 4" of 3-stitch I-cord, leaving 6" tails at both ends, and tie a Celtic knot for the top of the hat. Use the ends to sew the knot to the hat.

Hat Chart

29
28
27
26
25
24
23
22
21
20
19
18
17
16
15
14
13
12
11
10
9
8
7
6
5
4
3
2
1

2 —> 16 -st repeat

☐ K on RS, p on WS
▨ P on RS, k on WS
↓ K1b on RS, p1b on WS
▨ P1b on RS, k1b on WS
☑ Sl 1 wyif on RS
☑ Sl 1 wyif on WS
▼ Double increase
☐ Stitches worked in pattern before increase

Celtic Knot

Row 1 (RS) With A, k1, *k1b, k1; repeat from *, slide.
Row 2 (RS) With B, k1, * k1, k1b; repeat from *, end k2, turn.
Row 3 (WS) With A, p1, *p1b, p1; repeat from *, slide.
Row 4 (WS) With B, p1, *p1, p1b; repeat from *, end p2, turn.
Repeat rows 1–4 for Column Pattern.

Column Pattern

2-st repeat

☐ K on RS, p on WS
⬇ K1b on RS, p1b on WS

Tattersall Scarf

EASY+

56" x 8½"
(without fringe)

10cm/4"
40
12
• over Column Pattern

1 2 3 **4** 5 6

Medium weight
A • 200 yds
C • 95 yds

1 2 **3** 4 5 6

Light weight
B • 175 yds

4.5 mm/US 7, or size to obtain
gauge, 60cm (24") or longer

Any size

&

Tapestry needle

*2 balls each NORO Silk Garden in color
226 (A), BLUE SKY ALPACAS Melange
in color 800 Cornflower (B), and 1 ball
BERROCO Ultra Silk in color 6106 (C)*

Notes
1 See *Techniques*, page 138, for long-tail loop cast-on, k1b, p1b, weaving, fringe, overhand knot, and slide.
2 Work edge stitches firmly.

Scarf
With A and using long-tail loop cast-on, cast on 165 stitches. Join B at tail-end of needle and purl across row (A and B are at same end of needle); turn. Work Column Pattern, rows 1–4, 18 times, then work rows 1–3, EXCEPT at end of row 3, do not slide; turn. Cut B only; do not cut A.
Edging With RS facing, A, and loop cast-on, cast 2 stitches onto left needle. **Row 1** (RS) P1, p2tog (1 edging stitch together with 1 scarf stitch). **Row 2** (WS) P2. Repeat rows 1–2 until 2 stitches remain. Bind off.
With RS facing, slip needle into cast-on loops of scarf—164 stitches. Join A and work Edging.

Finishing
Block scarf, stretching it gently. Sew in ends.
Woven strands Cut 13 pieces of C, each 20" longer than scarf. Hold the strands together at one end and trim to the same length. *With tapestry needle threaded with a length of C, work across the first B row, weaving over every A column and under every B column. Keep yarn relaxed, without pulling. Insert needle under both legs of the stitch, and leave 10" tail at each end. Repeat from * every third row (see photograph).
Fringe Cut 52 pieces of C, each 20" long. Hold 2 lengths together and with hook draw through 'ditch' between the edge stitch and the first pattern stitch at each woven tail. Align ends and tie in an overhand knot to combine fringe and woven strands. Trim fringe.

TIP The following optional step facilitates finishing. Make a butterfly with 16 yards of yarn as the tail for the cast-on of the scarf. By preparing this tail, there is no need to attach a new piece of yarn when the lower edging has to be worked. You can pin the butterfly to the work so it doesn't get in the way as you knit the scarf.

The long sides of the scarf are finished with a 2-stitch sideways garter edging.

Column Pattern OVER AN ODD NUMBER OF STITCHES
Row 1 (RS) With A, k2, *k1, k1b; repeat from *, end k3, slide.
Row 2 (RS) With B, p2, *k1b, k1; repeat from *, end k1b, p2, turn.
Row 3 (WS) With A, p2, *p1, p1b; repeat from *, end p3, slide.
Row 4 (WS) With B, k2, *p1b, p1; repeat from .* end p1b, k2, turn.
Repeat rows 1–4 for Column Pattern.

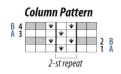

Column Pattern

2-st repeat

☐ K on RS, p on WS
▨ P on RS, k on WS
↓ K1b on RS, p1b on WS

Inside-Outside Scarf

Note

1 See *Techniques*, page 138, for long-tail loop cast-on, k1b, p1b, purl loop bind-off, slide. **2** Work from the inside of one ball (color A) and from the outside of a second ball (color B). **3** To tidy edge, after working the first stitch of rows 1 and 3 with color A, insert needle into next stitch, then give color B a little tug before completing the stitch with A.

Scarf

With A and using long-tail loop cast-on, cast on 19 stitches. Purl 3 rows. Work rows 1–4 of Column Pattern (joining B on row 2) to approximately 50" or desired scarf length, ending with a WS B row (row 4 of pattern) and leaving just enough B to work 1 more row plus bind-off (at least 6 times the width of the scarf). With B, purl one row, then with WS facing, bind off using purl loop bind-off. Sew in ends. Block.

EASY+

Approximately 6" × 50" or larger

10cm/4"

32

12

• over Column Pattern

1 2 3 **4** 5 6

Medium weight
A & B • 110 yds each
Optional: allow extra for fringe

6mm/US 10, or size to obtain gauge, 60cm (24") or longer

&
Tapestry needle

From left to right:
3 balls NASHUA HANDKNITS Vignette in Dusk #12
2 balls NORO Kureyon in Color 92
3 balls SKACEL/ZITRON Loft Color in Royal Multi Colored #910
2 balls NASHUA HANDKNITS Wooly Stripes in Jewels #26

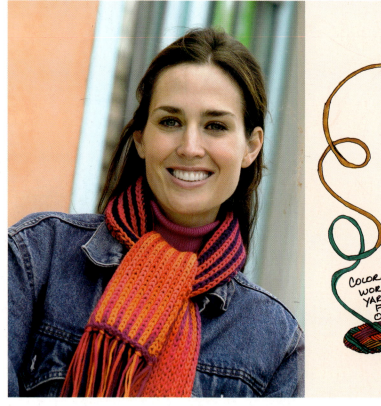

COLOR B WORK YARN FROM OUTSIDE

COLOR A WORK YARN FROM INSIDE

Pick two balls of long-repeat yarn, work one from the inside and one from the outside in the versatile Column Pattern. You'll have an exciting, reversible scarf.

Beading Pattern

Note Place bead by sliding bead between two stitches, do not pull bead through the stitch itself.
Round 1 With A, knit. *Round 2* With A, purl. *Round 3* With B, knit. *Round 4* With B, *p1, place bead, p1; repeat from *—40 stitches.

Ruffle 1 OVER AN EVEN NUMBER OF STITCHES
Round 1 With A, *k3, k1b; repeat from *.
Round 2 With B, *p1, p1b, p2; repeat from *.

Ruffle 1

4-st repeat

Ruffle 2 OVER AN ODD NUMBER OF STITCHES
Round 1 With A, *k2, k1b; repeat from *.
Round 2 With B, *p1b, p2; repeat from *.

Ruffle 2
3-st repeat

☐ Knit
▨ Purl
☑ K1b
▨ P1b

BEGINNER +

Adult woman

10cm/4"
48/40
24/20
• over garter stitch

1 2 **3** 4 5 6
Light weight
Toppers • 85 yds
Wristers • 80 yds

1 2 3 **4** 5 6
Medium weight
Toppers • 75 yds

2.25 mm / US1
3.25 mm / US3
or size to obtain gauge

&

400 beads (size 6), tapestry needle, stitch markers, and yarn needle

Sock Yarn:
Topper 1 skein Black and 1 skein White
Topper 1 skein each KOIGU Kersti in solid and in variegated
Wrister 1 ball each REGIA Silk sock yarn in color 90 and Silk Shine sock yarn in color 198
Wrister 1 skein FLEECE ARTIST Hand-dyed Woolie Silk 3-ply in color Sugar Plum

Toppers & Wristers

Notes

1 See *Techniques,* page 138, for double-loop cast-on, long-tail cast-on, k1b, p1b, slide, YO bind-off, and working with dpns. See page 74 for working with beads. *2* Instructions for wristlets are for 2 yarns; if using only one yarn, ignore A and B designations. *3* For stringing and placing beads, see page 74. *4* Reverse A and B colors on the second wristlet.

THIN & THICK TOPPERS

With A and using double-loop cast-on, cast on 40 (48) stitches. End extra strand of A. Slide. Join B at non-tail end of needle, and knit 1 round. Divide stitches evenly over 3 or 4 dpns. Join and mark beginning of round. With B, purl 1 round. With A, knit 1 round, purl 1 round. With B, knit 1 round, purl 1 round. Repeat last 4 rounds for 4" or longer, end with a B purl round.
Ruffle
Increase round for thin topper With A, * yo, k1; repeat from *—96 stitches. With B, purl 1 round.
Increase round for thick topper With A, *k1, yo, k1; repeat from *—60 stitches. With B, purl 1 round.
Work in **Ruffle 1** OR **2** for 1", end with A round. With WS facing and A, work YO bind-off knitwise. Sew in ends.

WRISTERS

String 200 beads onto A yarn and 200 beads onto B yarn (or 400 beads on one yarn).
With A and using long-tail loop cast-on, cast on 40 stitches. Divide stitches evenly over 3 or 4 dpns. Join and mark beginning of round. Work Beading Pattern, beginning with round 2, until you have 16 garter ridges (8 bead rounds), end after a bead round (round 4 of pattern). **Increase round** With A, *yo, k1; repeat from *—80 stitches. With B, purl 1 round. Work Ruffle 1 for 1", end with A round. **Next round** With B, *p1, p1b, p1, k1: repeat from *. With Color A, bind off as follows: Cast on 1 stitch onto left needle. *Place bead, (p2tog, slip stitch back to left needle) 3 times, place bead, p2tog, slip stitch back to left needle; repeat from *. Continue until all stitches have been bound off; pull yarn through last stitch. Sew in ends.

Top those boots!
Warm those wrists!
Add pizazz with ruffles
and beads.

K1b and Socks

The pinwheel sock pattern gives you choices: 4 cuffs, 3 stitch counts and 2 toes (with and without jog) as well as a one-yarn (odd numbers of stitches) and a 2-yarn version (even numbers of stitches). The sideways garter-stitch edge is a nice way to start a k1b sock, 40 sideways ridges is just right for an adult sock, 40 columns can be picked up from the side of the garter strip. Worked in two colors, the Columns will grow right out of the striped garter strip.

Create a hybrid sock where the cuff and leg of the hybrid socks use any of the k1b options. Then work the foot of your favorite sock pattern, simply increasing from the 40 stitches to 60 (or 64 or whatever number of stitches you would like to use). Work a few rounds of stockinette stitch (or whatever you choose) over the larger number of stitches for the ankle, then continue with the heel and foot of your choice. There are so many sock patterns out there, and everyone has a technique they like to use. So make your own hybrids.

Tofutsie yarn in the k1b pattern produces little specks and V-shapes, looking nothing like stockinette stitch.

Combine Kaffe Fassett Regia yarn, Mirage (A), with Landscape (B). Colors don't repeat very often. The bright blue only shows up once in the leg and once near the toe, and the dark red band only appears once around the ankle. Some knitters are perfectly willing to let the stripes fall where they may, but start the self-striping yarn in the same place for both socks for true mates!

You can also see the jog-free transitions in the heels and toes.

Mirage and Landscape worked over the same amount of stitches at a tighter gauge yields a pleasing pair of socks that will be a nice fit for a woman with a medium-sized foot.

This cabled sock uses the same cable as the Yin Yang man's cardigan. Navy and white showcase the cable, but two solid colors with less contrast would also be attractive. Jog-free heels and toes are simple—a perfect use for k1b stitch.

Why K1b for Socks?

- Thanks to the stretch inherent in the stitch pattern, k1b socks accommodate the leg and gently hug the foot.
- Sizing is easy: only 3 stitch counts necessary—40 stitches fits adults, 36 stitches fits children and 32 stitches fits babies. Varying the lengths of the leg and foot is the only size adjustment necessary (39, 35, and 31 respectively when working with a single yarn in k1b).
- The cuff treatments all stretch and slip easily over the foot.
- Self-striping sock yarns are a wonderful addition to the world. But in a conventional sock pattern in which the heel is worked as you shape, the heel can interfere with the continuity of the stripes. By working the heel at a later point in time, the stripes flow uninterrupted from the cuff to the toe.
- One self-striping yarn in a project stipples or speckles the color changes along the rounds.
- Working one self-striping yarn on an odd number of stitches is rather painless as you just flow k1, k1b, round and round in a spiral until desired length.
- Working with self-striping sock yarn is great fun, but after a while stockinette stitch becomes a bit predictable. Combine the stripes with a solid and extend the bands of color, totally changing their appearance in a sock.
- Working self-striping yarn with a second yarn in Column Pattern requires an even number of stitches.
- The jog-free option is a good solution when two highly contrasting colors are used, whereas when the colors are similar, the heel and toe can be worked without this technique.
- The garter construction of the pinwheel heel and toe provides extra cushion and durability while wrapping nicely around the foot.
- By working 1 k1b stitch after the first round of a new color, you eliminate the jog of the color transition. And of course, this technical trick is also quite useful for any garter-stitch project where the knitter wants to create neat color transitions between striped rounds.
- An adult sock knit with 6-ply sock yarn requires 36 stitches rather than 40 stitches.

Socks

Size	Baby	Child	Adult
Length of foot	5-6"	7-8"	9-11"
Length of leg of sock	2½-3½"	4-6"	7-9"
Number of stitches to be cast-on for 1-yarn/2yarn sock	31/32	35/36	39/40
Number of stitches for garter heel and toe	48	52	60
Length of foot before starting toe	2-3"	3-5"	5-7"
Number of rounds for heel and toe	22	24	28

One Yarn: Odd Number of Stitches

Regia Stretch is a good choice for socks using the k1b pattern. The Lycra produces a nice and snug fit. Since the color changes are quite short, the fabric ends up looking speckled—certainly quite different from stockinette stitch fabric.

An adorable kids' sock features ruffles and pinwheel shaping.

In this yarn, short color bursts occur every so many yards. These colors would stripe in stockinette, but form a line of stipples instead in k1b. The garter-stitch band is 52 ridges, and decreases to 39 stitches for the sock body. Can't find this yarn? Use a solid in the k1b pattern and insert an occasional round of bright color.

K1b socks are made in a yarn with fairly short color changes. The stockinette swatch was knit circularly to show how a typical 60-stitch sock would look. The simpler pinwheel heel and toe are used because there is no visible jog with this yarn.

To add a traditional stockinette foot and heel flap to a Column Pattern sock, increase from 40 to 60 stitches at the ankle. Work the heel stitch pattern by slipping 1 out of 3 stitches in order to continue the blue vertical lines.

Regia Silk sock wool in two solid colors clearly shows the striping and structure within the sock design. The pinwheel toe has perfect garter ridges thanks to the k1b jogless construction.

2 Solids Together

A hybrid design combines the Column Pattern with a traditional hourglass heel. Mix a solid with a self-striping yarn for bands of color.

Two Yarns: Even Number of Stitches

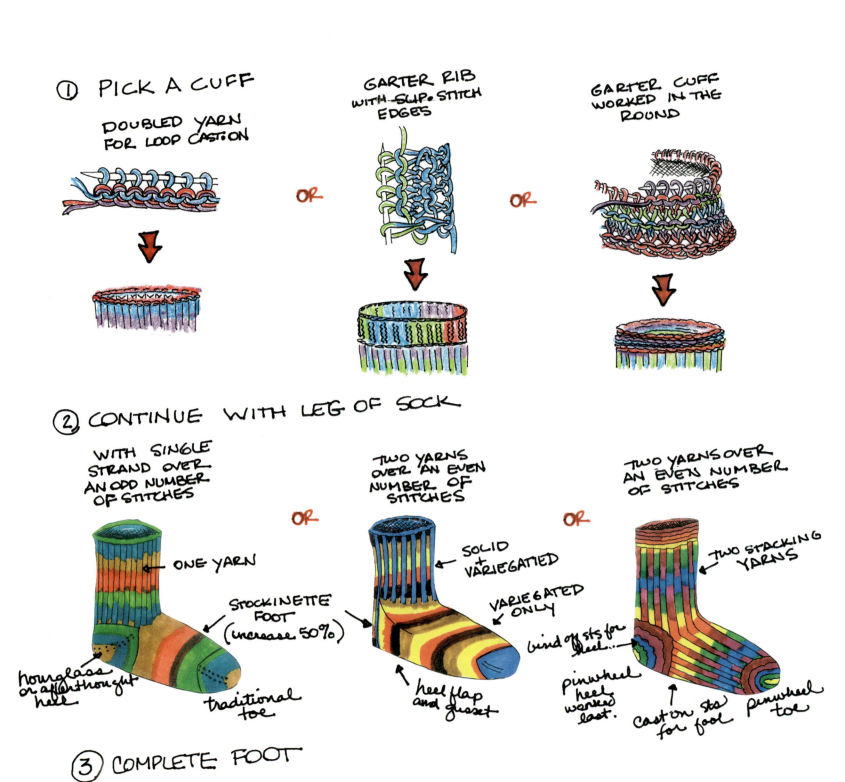

① PICK A CUFF

DOUBLED YARN FOR LOOP CAST-ON

GARTER RIB WITH ~~SLIP~~ STITCH EDGES

GARTER CUFF WORKED IN THE ROUND

OR

OR

② CONTINUE WITH LEG OF SOCK

WITH SINGLE STRAND OVER AN ODD NUMBER OF STITCHES

TWO YARNS OVER AN EVEN NUMBER OF STITCHES

TWO YARNS OVER AN EVEN NUMBER OF STITCHES

OR

OR

ONE YARN

STOCKINETTE FOOT (increase 50%)

hourglass or afterthought heel

traditional toe

SOLID + VARIEGATED

VARIEGATED ONLY

heel flap and gusset

TWO STACKING YARNS

bind off sts for heel...

pinwheel heel worked last.

cast on sts for foot

pinwheel toe

③ COMPLETE FOOT

Circular Column Pattern OVER AN EVEN NUMBER OF STITCHES (2 YARNS)
Round 1 (RS) With A, *k1, k1b; repeat from *.
Round 2 (RS) With B, *k1b, k1; repeat from *.

Circular K1b Pattern OVER AN ODD NUMBER OF STITCHES (1 YARN)
Round 1 (RS) *K1, k1b; repeat from *, end k1.
Round 2 (RS) *K1b, k1; repeat from *, end k1b.

Circular Column Pattern

2-st repeat

Circular K1b Pattern

2-st repeat

☐ K on RS
☑ K1b on RS

Pinwheel Socks

INTERMEDIATE

Baby (Child, Adult)
Foot circumference 4–5 (6–7, 7–8)"
Total foot length 4–5 (6–8, 9–11)"
(back of heel to tip of toe)

10cm/4"

60
20

• over Column Pattern Stitch
• For convenience, work gauge
swatch back and forth, following
Column Pattern on page 4.

1 **2** 3 4 5 6

Fine weight
A • 100 (250, 350) yds

Five 2.25mm/US 1 or size to
obtain gauge

&

Stitch markers, yarn needle,
waste yarn

Notes
1 See *Techniques*, page 138, for double loop cast-on, long-tail loop cast-on, loop cast-on, k1b, M1, and working with dpns. **2** Work change-over from yarn A to yarn B at beginning of round loosely and do not twist the yarns when you change color. **3** Instructions are for 2 yarns; if using only one yarn, ignore A and B designations. **4** The leg and foot of the 2-yarn sock are worked over an even number of stitches (shown in red); the leg and foot of the 1-yarn sock are worked over an odd number of stitches (shown in blue). Toes and heels for both are worked over 48 (54, 60) stitches.

Purl ridge cuff
With A and using double loop cast-on, cast on 32 (36, 40) 31 (33, 39) stitches. Join a single strand of B at tail-end of needle and purl across row (A and B are now at same end of needle). Distribute stitches over 3 or 4 dpn. Join and mark beginning of round. With A, knit 1 round. Begin Column Pattern with Round 2.

Garter ridge cuff
Cast on 6 stitches. *__Row 1__(RS) Slip 1, k5. **Row 2** (WS) Slip 1, k5. Repeat from * for a total of 31 (35, 39) times. Work Row 1 once more, then graft first row to last. With A, pick up and knit 1 stitch per ridge around—32 (36, 40) stitches. Distribute stitches over 3 or 4 dpn. Join and mark beginning of round. Begin Column Pattern with Round 2.

Garter stitch cuff
With A and using long-tail loop cast-on, cast on 48 (54, 60) 47 (53, 59) stitches. Distribute stitches over 3 or 4 dpn. Join, and mark beginning of round. Purl 1 round. With B, knit 1 round, purl 1 round. With A, knit 1 round, purl 1 round. With B, knit 1 round, purl one round. With A, knit 1 round. **Decrease round** With B, [k2tog, k1] 16 (18, 20) times—32 (36, 40) stitches. Begin Column Pattern with Round 1 (for a single yarn, decrease 1 stitch at beginning of round)—32 (36, 40) 31 (35, 39) stitches.

Ruffled cuff
With A and using long-tail loop cast-on, cast on 184 (208, 232) stitches, turn. Knit across row. Distribute stitches over 3 or 4 dpn. Join, and mark beginning of round. Purl 1 round. **Decrease round 1** With B, k2tog across row—92 (104, 116) stitches. Purl 1 round. Repeat last 2 rounds with A—46 (52, 58) stitches. **Decrease round 3** With B, k1, [k2tog, k1] 14 (16, 18) 15 (17, 19) times, end k3 (K0)—32 (36, 40) 31 (35, 39) stitches. Begin Column Pattern with Round 1.

Leg

Work Column Pattern until leg measures 3 (5, 7)" or desired length, end with a B round.

Heel preparation

Note The heel will be worked after the rest of the sock is finished.

With A, work 17 (19, 21) 16 (18, 20) stitches in pattern for top of foot, slip next 15 (17, 19) stitches onto waste yarn for heel. Continuing with A, cast on 15 (17, 19) stitches loosely using loop cast-on method (any other cast-on will be too tight). **Next round** With B, work 17 (19, 21) 16 (18, 20) stitches in pattern, knit 15 (17, 19) cast-on stitches—32 (36, 40) 31 (35, 39) stitches.

Foot

Work all stitches in pattern until piece measures 2½ (4½, 6)" from heel cast-on, or until 3 (3½, 4)" less than desired length, end after a B round.

Pinwheel Toe

Notes 1 Toes and heels for both 1-yarn and 2-yarn socks are worked over an even number of stitches. For 1-yarn socks, M1 at beginning of round 1. **2** For all sizes, set up on rounds 1 & 2; for baby, work rounds 11–28; for child work rounds 9–28; for adult work rounds 3–28.

Jog-free Pinwheel Toe & Heel At the end of each odd-numbered round, work to the marker, remove it, work a k1b, then replace the marker one stitch to the left. This prevents the 'jog' that would otherwise appear at the transitions of the rounds.

Baby and (Adult) Only **Round 1** With A, [work 1 stitch in pattern, M1, work 1 stitch in pattern] 16 (0, 20) times—48 (60) stitches.

Round 2 With A, purl.

Child sock only **Round 1** With B, *[work 1 stitch in pattern, M1, work 1 stitch in pattern] 8 times, work 2 in pattern. Repeat from *—52 stitches.

Round 2 With B, purl. Continue with row 9.

Adult sock only

Round 3 With B, *k60. **Round 4 and all even-numbered rounds** Purl with color used in previous round.

Round 5 With A, [k**13**, k2tog] 4 times,—56 stitches. **Round 7** With B, [k**12**, k2tog] 4 times,—52 stitches.

Adult & Child

Round 9 With A, [k**11**, k2tog] 4 times—48 stitches.

All socks

Round 11 With B, [k**10**, k2tog] 4 times—**44** stitches. **Round 13** With A, [k**9**, k2tog] 4 times—**40** stitches.

Round 15 With B, [k**8**, k2tog] 4 times—**36** stitches. **Round 17** With A, [k**7**, k2tog] 4 times—**32** stitches.

Round 19 With B, [k**6**, k2tog] 4 times.—**28** stitches. **Round 21** With A, [k**5**, k2tog] 4 times—**24** stitches.

Round 23 With B, [k**4**, k2tog] 4 times—**20** stitches. **Round 25** With A, [k**3**, k2tog] 4 times—**16** stitches.

Round 27 With B, [k**2**, k2tog] 4 times—**12** stitches. **Round 28** With B, purl.

Cut yarns and run tails through remaining stitches. Pull tightly and secure.

Pinwheel Heel

Place 15 (17, 19) stitches from waste yarn onto dpn.

Round 1 With A, *work 1 stitch in pattern, M1, work 1 stitch in pattern; repeat from*, work last stitch in pattern—22 (25, 28) stitches. Continue with A, pick up and knit 26 (27, 32) stitches evenly along cast-on edge—48 (52, 60) stitches.

Rounds 2 to 28 Work as for toe, beginning Baby sock on Round 9, Child sock on Round 7, and Adult sock on Round 2.

Like Yin & Yangs — cables & stripes worked in two solids! In high contrast yarns, the pinwheel incorporates a k1b to hide the jog.

2-YARN SOCK WITH CABLES

The pattern consists of a left-cross 3-stitch cable. One cable is worked in the 7th round with Color A, creating a cable in Color B. The other cable is worked in the 8th round with Color B, creating a cable in Color A. The first and third stitches of the cable cross in front of the center stitch, which continues straight up the center.

1/1/1 Left Cross (1/1/1 LC)

Slip 1 stitch to cable needle, hold to front; slip 1 stitch to another cable needle, hold to back, k1; k1 from back cable needle; k1 from front cable needle: the first and third stitches cross left over right in front of the center stitch.

Circular Column Pattern with Cables

Rounds 1, 3, 5 With A, *k1, k1b; repeat from *. *Rounds 2, 4, 6* With B, *k1b, k1; repeat from *.
Round 7 With A, 1/1/1 Left Cross, * work 2 stitches in pattern, slip 1 stitch to cable needle and hold at front, slip 1 stitch to another cable needle and hold at back, k1, k1 from back cable needle, k1 from front cable needle, work 11 (13, 15) stitches in pattern; repeat from *.
Round 8 With B, 1/1/1/ Left Cross, * work 11 (13, 15) stitches in pattern, slip 1 stitch to cable needle and hold at front, slip 1 stitch to another cable needle and hold at back, k1, k1 from back cable needle, k1 from front cable needle, work 2 stitches in pattern; repeat from *.
Repeat Rounds 1–8.

Socks

Work Purl Ridge Cuff for 32 (36, 40) stitches. Work leg and top of foot in Circular Column Pattern with Cables. Work bottom of foot in Circular Column Pattern without cables. Work Pinwheel Toes and Heels or Jog-free Pinwheel Toes and Heels.

Stashbusters

To prevent the house from bursting at the seams, we need stashbusters. The Starry Night Shawl, the Red Afghan, the Blue Afghan, and the Fringe Benefits Vest show just a few ways to use up your treasures.

Fringe Benefits Vest

This project was a lot of fun. A little vest is a good garment to play with as you venture into uncharted color territory. Fringe Benefits combines a large number of different yarns, divided into two categories: Color A (thick reds) and Color B (thin mixed colors). Every row is knit with a different yarn and the strand is cut at the end of each row. The ends are knotted into a decorative fringe that flips neatly to the inside when the stitches are picked up for garter-stitch bands. Even if the vest blows open, you won't mind if the fringe shows (see photo, page ix).

Any of the vest patterns in this book can be the launching point for a stash vest. Pick one with a gauge that is similar to your stash swatch (see Gauge, page 134). Since every row changes the appearance of your work, the suspense will keep you going, you will often find yourself saying "Just one more row," and before you know it, you'll be finished.

Laid-Back Lapels (page 14) would be a good choice since the fringe becomes the trim for the lapels. Or how about a really easy vest with no borders at all? Just let the trimmed fringe form the edging along the fronts and armholes.

The East-Meets-West Jacket (page 36) could also be made in a fringed version. Simply skip the garter-stitch edging along the panels and off you go. Or how about a scarf with short, trimmed fringe running down the sides? Showcase those favorite yarns, take the plunge, and have a good time.

Color selection

'Stash' does not necessarily mean 'oddball'. After all, we want our stash projects to look as if we had designed them rather than used up our leftovers. A project made of a bit of this and a bit of that can look busy and non-cohesive. It is a good idea to avoid too many different colors and to make sure that there is a dominant shade. Since the Column Pattern alternates equal amounts of Colors A and B, it lends itself quite well for working with two groups of colors, preventing the project from looking like a motley crew of odds and ends.

A good approach is to apply the 50-percent formula. If Color A columns comprise one color (or family of similar colors), then the color B columns can get away with including a greater mix of contrasting fibers and colors. A somewhat monochromatic range for one set of columns gives the project continuity, allowing the other columns to feature diverse colors and textures. This gives you freedom to be bold and indulge in color creativity, and yet the result will be pleasing to the eye, lively but harmonious. There is no hard-and-fast order in which to place the yarns. In fact, it is often visually more interesting if you do not establish a regular sequence. Just pick a yarn from your A group and then one from your B group.

Many excellent publications have delved into the color wheel, discussing primary, secondary, and complementary colors. Rather than approaching your color choices from a theoretical standpoint, I encourage you to look at your options and create groups of colors that are agreeable to you. Look for pleasing colors around you—in nature, in your favorite pictures, everywhere—and group your yarns accordingly, or choose a favorite color range and play it against a neutral color such as white or grey, or juxtapose various bright colors against black. In a pinch, break the 'stash rules' and buy a bit of yarn to fill a gap in your palette.

Yarn selection

You will also be deciding on yarns. Here again, you have considerable latitude. These projects do not have to be made of a single type or weight of yarn. You can mix fibers and textures: the Fringe Benefits Vest contains mostly wool and a bit of rayon, silk, cotton, acrylic, alpaca, as well as blends in a wide variety of textures and thicknesses.

Adding to your design freedom is the fact that yarn thickness is of no concern here. The Red Afghan uses yarns ranging from very thin to very thick. When you come across a thin yarn, simply hold two strands together; they do not even have to be the same color. If you have just worked a row with a fairly thin yarn, select a thicker one for the next row. The heavier yarn will 'share' the space, spilling over into the area around the thinner yarn and keeping your fabric uniform.

Your group A and group B yarns can also differ in terms of texture rather than color. If the A yarns are thicker than the B yarns, all the better. You will add a dimension of thick-and-thin, peaks-and-valleys to the texture, producing a supple and three-dimensional fabric.

Beginnings and endings

The stash projects presented here were all cast on over an odd number of stitches with the long-tail loop cast-on. This cast-on has just the right width to serve as a good base for the Column Pattern and the odd number of stitches ensures that the two columns at the outer edges will be of the same color. The upper and lower borders of the afghans are worked after the piece is finished. By the time you have completed an afghan, you will have developed an opinion as to which yarns you would like to use for the borders. Adding such borders does away with the need to bind off in the usual manner and provides an edging along the top and bottom of the piece that is far more substantial than any cast-on and bind-off would be.

Selvedges

The selvedges of the afghans and the vest are worked as fringe. At the end of each row, cut the yarn with a tail ranging from 3" to 8" and slide the knitting back to the beginning of the needle. All these projects can be worked exclusively on the right side: no purl or p1b stitches have to be worked, and the pattern repeat is a mere two rows. Cut the yarns and tie with overhand knots. With the fringe approach, there is no need to weave in the many ends. You could also use a sewing machine to make 2 or 3 rows of very small stitches to anchor all the ends, trimming them for a short fringe.

In the Starry Night Shawl (page 137), the yarns are carried loosely up the selvedges. Then the sides are finished with a row of single crochet worked in mohair, 'wrapping' the carried yarns and stabilizing the edges.

Gauge

It is perhaps knitting heresy to say that gauge does not matter, but in a project such as the afghans, the most important aspect is that you create a fabric that is pleasing to the hand. If you have a range of yarns of different thickness, pick a knitting needle that matches one of the yarns in the middle of the weight range and use that one to make a swatch. This will also give you a chance to check if you like your color choices. After that, cast on lots of stitches and go for it!

Weaving

After you have finished your afghan, you can weave yarns over the columns, a technique that shows off accent yarns to great advantage, while contributing to stability, warmth, and texture. By weaving an A yarn over A columns, the effect is quite subtle, as can be seen in the Red Afghan (page 137). A plaid effect is achieved by weaving A over B columns, as in the Blue Afghan. You can space these woven yarns at random or you can distribute them evenly over your fabric. Weave a bright color to enliven a muted section of your work.

Cut pieces of yarn that are about 12" longer than the width of the piece. With a large tapestry needle, weave these yarns across the afghan, leaving 6" tails to be incorporated into the fringe. As you weave, just slip the tapestry needle under the two legs of the stitch and the weaving will not be visible on the reverse side of the afghan.

The Blue Afghan

We all have a skein or two of something special in our stashes that we would like to showcase. For instance, I had a skein of hand-dyed, hand-spun yarn made by a friend from the wool of her own sheep and a skein of merino hand-dyed by another friend. This afghan provided a way to highlight these special yarns in a large project. It is made with five skeins of light gray worsted weight wool as Color A and five skeins of other colors (a light blue, a pink, a medium blue, and my two special skeins) as Color B. The readily available commercial yarn is the canvas on which to paint with the beautiful hand-spun and hand-dyed yarns.

Blue Afghan Border

Since this afghan started off with a long-tail loop cast-on, it needed borders at the upper and lower edges that would be as wide and flexible as the Column Pattern. By adding the borders last, your top and bottom finishes will match each other precisely. And you won't run the risk that your initially chosen edging turns out to be too tight or too loose, long after you can easily go back and correct it. There was a need for something that would be firm enough to form a sturdy border for the beginning and end of this afghan. The solution here was a sort of purled I-cord that is looser than a conventional I-cord. It makes neat little ridges because the edging is wrapped so to speak when you bring the yarn forward, adding a bit of volume to the border.

Once your afghan is as big as you'd like it to be, leave the stitches on the needle. With the yarn you have selected for the border and with RS facing, work 2 stitches in Column Pattern, increase 1 by picking up the crossbar without twisting it, thus creating one stitch between the second and third columns. Continue this all the way across, cut the yarn, and slide the stitches back to beginning of needle. You will now have about one-and-a-half times as many stitches as you had originally cast on. With the same color yarn, loop cast-on 3 stitches; *p2, p2tog, take yarn to back, slip 3 stitches back to left needle, bring yarn forward; repeat from * until 3 stitches remain, p3tog, pull yarn through and incorporate the tail into the fringe. For a narrower band, work this same edging over 2 stitches rather than over 3 stitches.

Starry Night Shawl

This stash project is also worked back and forth in the Column Pattern. But this time, the yarns are not cut at the ends of the row but rather are carried loosely up the sides of the shawl. It is made of only four yarns; a mohair (Color A) and three fancy yarns containing cotton, rayon, linen, mohair, acrylic, polyamide, and metallic fibers (B1, B2, B3). Since these last three yarns are changed every B row, the yarns are carried only a short distance. You work in the usual Column Pattern consisting of two RS rows and two WS rows. The fact that you switch your B color each time does not interfere with this rhythmic sequence.

Finishing is simple: once you've reached the desired length, add a row of single crochet in mohair along the lengthwise edges of the shawl, working one single crochet in the 'ditch' adjacent to each V. This will conceal the carried yarns. Then work a row of crochet chain stitches across the short ends before adding the fringe. Don't worry about sewing in ends when you crochet with the mohair. Just leave 8" tails hanging to be incorporated into the fringe. Follow the fringe instructions on page 143 and you're done. Ready for a glamorous Starry Night on the town.

The Red Afghan

This afghan was a great stashbuster. In fact, I bought no new yarn at all for it. As you can see from the fringe, many different yarns were used and their fiber content varied widely, wildly, and even wickedly. The grays are a fairly homogenous group of Shetland-type yarns in a few similar shades and weights. However, the 'red' stripes include many shades of red, some pink, purple, orange, maroon, and fuchsia in an assortment of textures, fiber contents, and yarn weights. If you were to look at a pile of these yarns, you would never think that the colors would work together. Yet once you have them distributed throughout the afghan, embedded in the tranquil gray columns, the colors don't clash. In fact, the many different hues and tones yield a depth that a single color could never attain. Once the afghan is finished, maroon and gray yarns are woven across the fabric every five rows to add a touch of horizontal color.

Red Afghan Border

The borders at the top and bottom of this afghan are really simple. Prepare for the border by increasing the number of stitches as described above for the Blue Afghan using a smaller needle. Alternating A and B, work 8 rows of reverse stockinette (purl across every row on the RS or, if you prefer, knit across every row on the WS), cutting yarn and leaving tails at beginning and end of each row to be incorporated into the fringe. Fold the band towards the back to make a hem and tack down the live stitches with a tapestry needle or crochet the stitches into place with a crochet hook. You'll have a nice rounded edge to finish off your project.

TECHNIQUES

KNIT, PURL IN ROW BELOW (k1b, p1b)

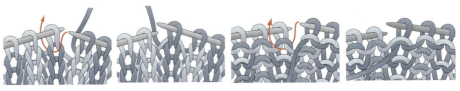

1 Instead of working into next stitch on left needle, work into stitch directly below it.
2 Pull stitch off left needles and let it drop.

CABLE CAST-ON

1 Start with a *slipknot* on left needle (first cast-on stitch). Insert right needle into slipknot from front. Wrap yarn over right needle as if to knit.

2 Bring yarn through slipknot, forming a loop on right needle.
3 Insert left needle in loop and slip loop off right needle. One additional stitch cast on.

4 Insert right needle **between** the last 2 stitches. From this position, knit a stitch and slip it to the left needle as in Step 3.
Repeat Step 4 for each additional stitch.

LONG-TAIL LOOP CAST-ON

1 Hold needle in left hand and tail of yarn in right hand (allowing about 1" for each stitch to be cast on).
2 Bring right index finger under yarn, pointing toward you.

3 Turn index finger to point away from you.
4 Insert tip of needle under yarn on index finger (see above); remove finger and draw yarn snug, forming a stitch.
Repeat Steps 2–4. After every few stitches, allow the yarn to hang freely to restore its original twist.

Loops can be formed over index or thumb.

LOOP CAST-ON

Used to cast-on stitches with the working yarn. Work as for long-tail loop cast-on EXCEPT do not use tail of yarn.

DOUBLE LOOP CAST-ON

1 Allowing a tail of about 1½" for each stitch to be cast on, fold yarn and make a double half-hitch on needle (as shown). These 2 loops count as 1 stitch and will be worked together on next row.

2 Holding tail and working yarn together and using loop cast-on, continue to cast on required number of stitches.

SLIDE

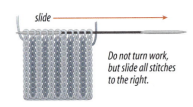

slide

Do not turn work, but slide all stitches to the right.

KOK INCREASE (k1-yo-k1)

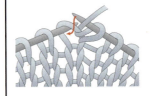

1 Knit 1, leaving stitch on left needle.
2 Bring yarn to front and over needle.
3 Knit into the stitch again.

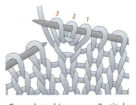

Completed increase: 3 stitches from 1 stitch.

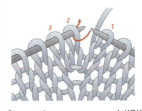

On next increase row, work KOK increase into center stitch of increase of previous increase row.

YO BIND-OFF

1 Knit 1 stitch as usual.
2 Yarn over.
3 With left needle, pass first stitch on right needle over the yarn-over…

… and off the needle.
4 Knit 1 more stitch.
5 Pass yarn-over over this knit stitch and off the needle (one stitch bound off).
Repeat Steps 1–5.

Note : Inserting a yarn-over between every 2 or 3 stitches rather than between every stitch gives you control over the amount of extra width you add to the bind-off.

3-NEEDLE YO BIND-OFF

1 With stitches on 2 needles, place *wrong sides together*.
* Knit 2 stitches together (1 from front needle and 1 from back needle.

2 *Yarn over, pass stitch on right needle over yarn-over and off right needle.

3 Knit next 2 stitches together, pass yarn-over over stitch and off needle.
4 Repeat Steps 2 and 3, end by drawing yarn through last stitch.

P2TOG BIND-OFF

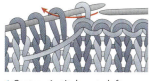

1 Cast on 1 stitch onto left needle, *p2tog. . .

. . . slip stitch back to left needle; repeat from *, end by drawing yarn through last stitch.

PURL LOOP BIND-OFF

Thread a length of yarn (at least 3 times the width of the knitted piece) in a tapestry needle. Tighten the bind-off as you work to match tension of cast-on.
1 Insert tapestry needle into second stitch *as if to purl* and pull through to the *front*, leaving stitch on knitting needle.

2 Insert tapestry needle into first stitch *as if to knit*, pull through, and drop stitch off knitting needle. Repeat Steps 1–2 until a single stitch remains. Insert tapestry needle into this stitch *as if to purl*.

FASTEN OFF

Work bind-off until only 1 stitch remains on right needle. If this is the last stitch of a row, cut yarn and fasten off stitch as shown above. Otherwise, this is the first stitch of the next section of knitting.

ZIGZAG BIND-OFF

With stitches on 2 needles, place *wrong sides together*, * bind off 1 stitch from front needle, bind off 1 stitch from back needle; repeat from *, end by drawing yarn through last stitch.

KNIT LOOP BIND-OFF

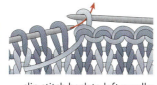

Work as Purl Loop Bind-off EXCEPT
1 Insert tapestry needle into second stitch *as if to knit* and pull through to the *back*, leaving stitch on knitting needle.

2 Insert tapestry needle into first stitch *as if to purl*, pull through, and drop stitch off knitting needle. Repeat Steps 1–2 until a single stitch remains. Insert tapestry needle into last stitch *as if to knit*.

BUTTON LOOP

Mark position for top and bottom of loop.
1 Bring yarn needle up at one marker and down at the other, creating a loop.

2 Bring yarn up at first marker once more.

3 Work buttonhole stitch around both loops as follows: bring yarn to left of needle, then bring needle under loops and over yarn. Pull through and tighten.

K2TOG BIND-OFF

K2, *insert left needle into 2 stitches on right needle and knit them together, k1; repeat from *, end by drawing yarn through last stitch.

ABBREVIATIONS

BO bind off
ch chain
cm centimeter(s)
CO cast on
– decreas(e)(ed)(es)(ing)
dec decreas(e)(ed)(es)(ing)
dpn double-pointed needle(s)
ER every row or round
EOR every other row or round
g gram(s)
" inch(es)
+ increas(e)(ed)(es)(ing)
inc increas(e)(ed)(es)(ing)
k knit(ting)(s)(ted)
k1b knit one below
k2tog knit 2 tog
k2togb knit 2 tog below
k3togb knit 3 tog below
LH left-hand
M1 Make one stitch (increase)
m meter(s)
mm millimeter(s)
oz ounce(s)
p purl(ed)(ing)(s) or page
p1b purl one below
pm place marker
psso pass slipped stitch(es) over
R row or round
RH right-hand
RS right side(s)
sc single crochet (UK double crochet)
sl slip(ped)(ping)
SSK slip, slip, knit 2 tog
SSKb slip below, slip, knit 2 tog
SSSKb slip below, slip, slip, knit 2 tog
SSP slip, slip, purl these 2 sts tog
st(s) stitch(es)
St st stockinette stitch
tog together
WS wrong side(s)
wyib with yarn in back
wyif with yarn in front
X times
yd(s) yard(s)
yo yarn over
   (UK yarn forward)

K2tog

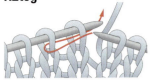

1 Insert right needle into first 2 stitches on left needle, beginning with second stitch from end of left needle.

2 Knit these 2 stitches together as if they were 1.
The result is a right-slanting decrease.

SSK

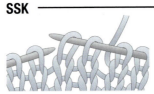

1 Slip 2 stitches *separately* to right needle as if to knit.

2 Slip left needle into these 2 stitches from left to right and knit them together: 2 stitches become 1.

The result is a left-slanting decrease.

P2tog

1 Insert right needle into first 2 stitches on left needle.

2 Purl these 2 stitches together as if they were 1.
The result is a right-slanting decrease.

SSP

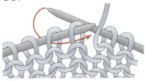

1 Work same as SSK Step 1.
2 Slip these 2 stitches back onto left needle. Insert right needle through their 'back loops,' into the second stitch and then the first.

3 Purl them together: 2 stitches become 1.

The result is a left-slanting decrease.

K2TOGb

1 Slip 1, slip 1 below as if to purl.

The result is 3 loops on right needle (1 color B stitch and 1 color A/B combo).

2 Place these 3 loops back onto left needle and knit them together.

The result is a right-slanting single decrease with color A on top of the 2 color B loops.

K3TOGb

Work same as K2togb EXCEPT:
1 Slip **2**, slip 1 below as if to purl.
The result is **4** loops on right needle.
2 Place these **4** loops back onto left needle and knit them together.
The result is a right-slanting **double** decrease.

SSKb

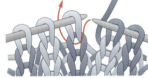

1a Slip 1 below as if to knit.

1b Slip 1 as if to knit.

The result is 3 loops on right needle (1 color A/B combo and 1 color B stitch).

2 Insert left needle from left to right into these 3 loops and knit them together.

The result is a left-slanting single decrease with color A on top of the 2 color B loops.

SSSKb

Work same as SSKb EXCEPT:
1a Slip 1 below as if to knit.
1b Slip **2** as if to knit.
The result is **4** loops on right needle.
2 Insert left needle from left to right into these **4** loops and knit them together.
The result is a left-slanting **double** decrease.

S2KP2, sl 2-k1-p2sso

1 Slip 2 stitches *together* to right needle as if to knit.

2 Knit next stitch.

3 Pass 2 slipped stitches over knit stitch and off right needle: 3 stitches become 1; the center stitch is on top.

The result is a centered double decrease.

DOUBLE INCREASE

  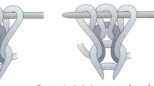

1 Knit into right side of stitch below the stitch on left needle.
2 Knit into the stitch on needle.
3 Knit into left side of stitch below (now 2 below).

One stitch is increased to three.

KNIT INTO FRONT AND BACK (kf&b)

1 Knit into the front of next stitch on left needle, but do not pull the stitch off the needle.
2 Take right needle to back, then knit through the back of the same stitch.

3 Pull stitch off left needle. Completed increase: 2 stitches from 1 stitch. This increase results in a purl bump after the knit stitch.

YARN OVER (yo)

Between knit stitches
Bring yarn under the needle to the front, take it over the needle to the back and knit the next stitch.

Completed yo increase.

PURL INTO FRONT AND BACK (pf&b)

1 Purl into front of next stitch, but do not pull stitch off needle.
2 Take right needle to back, then through back of same stitch, from left to right…

3 … and purl.

4 Pull stitch off left needle. Completed increase: 2 stitches from 1 stitch. This increase results in a purl bump before the stitch on the right side.

SLIP WITH YARN ON RIGHT SIDE OF WORK (wyif, wyib)

Move the yarn to the *front* on a right-side row…

… or to the *back* on a wrong-side row before slipping a stitch. This places the yarn on the right side of the fabric.

YO BUTTONHOLE

Row 1 (Right-side) Yarn over, k2tog (as shown).
Row 2 Purl into yarn-over.

MAKE 1 LEFT (M1L), KNIT

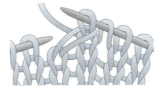 

Insert left needle from front to back under strand between last stitch knitted and first stitch on left needle. Knit, twisting strand by working into loop at back of needle.

Completed M1L knit: a left-slanting increase.

SLIP PURLWISE (sl 1 p-wise)

1 Insert right needle into next stitch on left needle from back to front (as if to purl).

2 Slide stitch from left to right needle. *Stitch orientation* does not change (right leg of stitch loop is at front of needle).

The stitch slipped purlwise can be a knit or a purl.

MAKE 1 RIGHT (M1R), KNIT

Insert left needle from back to front under strand between last stitch knitted and first stitch on left needle. Knit, twisting the strand by working into loop at front of the needle.

Completed M1R knit: a right-slanting increase.

SLIP KNITWISE (sl 1 k-wise)

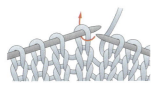  

1 Insert right needle into next stitch on left needle from front to back (as if to knit).

2 Slide stitch from left to right needle. *Stitch orientation* changes (right leg of stitch loop is at back of needle).

The stitch slipped knitwise can be a knit or a purl.

KNITTING IN ROUNDS

• After casting on, do not turn work. Knit into first cast-on stitch to join. Stop. Check to make sure that the cast-on does not spiral around the needle. If it does, undo the stitch, remove the spiral, then rejoin.
• Check your knitting at end of first and second rounds and make sure you have no twists.
• Mark the beginning of a round in one of three ways:
1 Place a marker on needle.
2 Use a safety pin in the fabric.
3 Weave your leftover cast-on tail between first and last stitch of round.

WORKING WITH 3 DOUBLE-POINTED NEEDLES (DPNS)

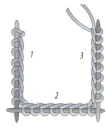
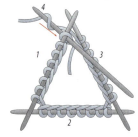

Cast stitches onto 1 dpn.
1 Rearrange stitches on 3 dpns. Check carefully that stitches are not twisted around a dpn or between dpns before beginning to work in rounds.

2 With a 4th dpn, work all stitches from first dpn. Use that empty dpn to work the stitches from the 2nd dpn. Use that empty dpn to work the stitches from the 3rd dpn—one round completed.

Place a marker between first and second stitch of first needle to mark beginning of round. Notice that you work with only 2 dpns at a time. As you work the first few rounds, be careful that the stitches do not twist between the needles.

WORKING WITH 4 DOUBLE-POINTED NEEDLES (DPNS)

If instructions recommend working with a set of 5 dpns, arrange the stitches on 4 needles and knit with the fifth.

INTARSIA - PICTURE KNITTING

Color worked in areas: each area is made with its own length of yarn. Twists made at each color change connect these areas.

Right-side row   *Wrong-side row*

Making a twist:

Work across row to color change, pick up new color from under the old and work across to next color change.

GRAFT IN GARTER

ON THE NEEDLES

1 Arrange stitches on 2 needles so stitches on lower, or front, needle come out of purl bumps and stitches on the upper, or back, needle come out of smooth knits.
2 Thread a blunt needle with matching yarn (approximately 1" per stitch).
3 Working from right to left, begin with Steps 3a and 3b:
3a Front needle: bring yarn through first stitch *as if to purl,* leave stitch *on needle.*
3b Back needle: repeat Step 3a.
4a Front needle: bring yarn through first stitch *as if to knit, slip off* needle; through next stitch *as if to purl, leave on* needle.
4b Back needle: repeat Step 4a.
Repeat Steps 4a and 4b until 1 stitch remains on each needle.
5a Front needle: bring yarn through stitch *as if to knit,* slip *off needle.*
5b Back needle: repeat Step 5a.
6 Adjust tension to match rest of knitting.

OFF THE NEEDLES

1 Place stitches on holding thread, remove needles, *block* pieces, and arrange so stitches on lower piece come out of purl bumps and stitches on the upper piece come out of smooth knits.
2 Thread a blunt needle with matching yarn (approximately 1" per stitch).
3 Working from right to left, begin with Steps 3a and 3b:
3a Lower piece: bring yarn from *back to front* through first stitch.
3b Upper piece: bring yarn from *front to back* through first stitch.
4a Lower piece: bring yarn from *front to back* through *previous stitch* worked, then from *back to front* through *next stitch.*
4b Upper piece: bring yarn from *back to front* through *previous stitch* worked, then from *front to back* through *next stitch*
Repeat Steps 4a and 4b until 1 stitch remains on each piece.
5a Lower piece: bring yarn from *front to back* through stitch.
5b Upper piece: bring yarn from *back to front* through stitch.
6 Remove holding thread and adjust tension to match rest of knitting.

BUTTERFLY

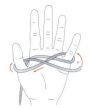

Butterfly wrap
Wrap yarn in figure-8 fashion around fingers. When finished, tuck end under last set of wraps, and free fingers.

Butterfly
Make small butterflies when using short lengths (less than 5 yards) of yarn for colorwork.

WORKING FROM CHARTS

Charts are graphs or grids of squares that represent the right side of knitted fabric. They illustrate every stitch and the relationship between the rows of stitches.
Squares contain knitting symbols.

The key defines each symbol as an operation to make a stitch or stitches.
The pattern provides any special instructions for using the chart(s) or the key.
The numbers along the sides of charts indicate the rows. A number on the right side marks a right-side row that is worked leftward from the number. A number on the left marks

a wrong-side row that is worked rightward. Since many stitches are worked differently on wrong-side rows, the key will indicate that. If the pattern is worked circularly, all rows are right-side rows and worked from right to left.
Bold lines within the graph represent repeats. These set off a group of stitches that are repeated across a row. You begin at the

edge of a row or where the pattern indicates for the required size, work across to the second line, then repeat the stitches between the repeat lines as many times as directed, and finish the row.
The sizes of a garment are often labeled with beginning and ending marks on the chart. This avoids having to chart each size separately.

CHAIN STITCH (ch st, ch)

1 Make a slipknot to begin.
2 Catch yarn and draw through loop on hook.

First chain made. Repeat Step 2.

SINGLE CROCHET (sc)

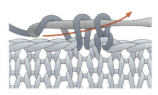

1 Insert hook into a stitch, catch yarn, and pull up a loop. Catch yarn and pull through the loop on the hook.
2 Insert hook into next stitch to the left.

3 Catch yarn and pull through the stitch; 2 loops on hook.

4 Catch yarn and pull through both loops on hook; 1 single crochet completed. Repeat Steps 2–4.

CRAB STITCH, BACKWARD SINGLE CROCHET

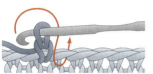

SLIP STITCH (sl st)

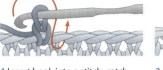

1 Insert hook into a stitch, catch yarn, and pull up a loop. Catch yarn and pull a loop through the loop on the hook.
2 Insert hook into next stitch to right.

3 Catch yarn and pull through stitch only (as shown). As soon as hook clears the stitch, flip your wrist (and the hook). There are 2 loops on the hook, and the just-made loop is to the front of the hook (left of the old loop).

4 Catch yarn and pull through both loops on hook; 1 backward single crochet completed.

5 Continue working to the right, repeating Steps 2–4.

Insert hook into the next stitch to the left, catch yarn and pull through both the stitch and the loop on the hook.

TASSELS

1 Wrap yarn around a piece of cardboard that is the desired length of the tassel. Thread a strand of yarn under the wraps, and tie it at the top, leaving a long end.

2 Cut the wrapped yarn at lower edge. Wrap the long end of yarn around upper edge and thread the yarn through the top as shown. Trim strands.

4-STRAND BRAID

Measure 4 strands of Color A and 4 strands of Color B that are twice as long as the cord needed. Tie these 8 strands together with an overhand knot, leaving 1" tails. Affix this to a doorknob or the like. Group 2 strands of the same color together, thus giving you 4 lengths that you wll be working with. Hold 2 lengths of A in your right hand and 2 lengths of B in your left.

1 Move the outside right-hand strand under two adjacent strands (toward the left) and back over one strand (toward the right). Pull tight.

2 Move the outside left-hand strand under two adjacent strands (toward the right) and back over one strand (toward the left). Pull tight.

Repeat steps 1 and 2.

I-CORD

Make a tiny tube of stockinette stitch with 2 double-pointed needles:
1 Cast on 3 or 4 sts.
2 Knit. Do not turn work. Slide stitches to opposite end of needle. Repeat Step 2 until cord is the desired length.

FRINGE

Cut lengths of yarn to twice desired length of fringe plus 1". Divide into groups of 2 or more strands.
1 Insert crochet hook from wrong side of work through a stitch at edge. Draw center of strands through, forming a loop.

2 Draw ends through loop. One fringe section complete.

WEAVING

Weave lengths of accent yarn or ribbon through a knitted fabric for interesting effects. Weave under both legs of the stitch; example shows inserting needle under 1 stitch and over 2 stitches.
Cut lengths of weaving yarn to the approximate required length (including extra length for fringe on each end). The base fabric will draw up as weaving continues. Smooth it out as you work to maintain width of knit fabric.

OVERHAND KNOT

SPLICING

Splicing eliminates the need to darn in ends when joining in a new skein of wool. Separate the plies of the last 3–4" of both the old end and the new skein. Break off (do not cut) half of the plies on each end.

Overlap two ends in one palm. Spit into your other palm and rub your hands together briskly until you can feel heat—about 15 seconds. This join will hold after it is knit into fabric; until then, avoid pulling on it.

LOOP SPLICING

Criss-cross the two yarns. Thread one yarn thought a sharp needle and fold back to form a loop. Weave the needle in and out back into the yarn, do the same with the second yarn weaving its tail into itself. NOTE: If your yarn it thick, break off a few plies of your yarn before you weave it in.

INSERTING ZIPPER

Sewing a zipper into a knit can seem daunting to the uninitiated. Although the knitted fabric has stretch, the zipper does not, and the two must be joined as neatly as possible to prevent ripples. Follow these steps for a smooth installation.

1 Measure the length of the opening. Select a zipper the length of the opening in the color of your choice. If you can't find that exact length, choose one that is a bit longer.

2 Pre-shrink your zipper in the method you will use to clean the garment. Wash and dry it or carefully steam it (you don't want to melt the teeth if they are plastic or nylon).

3 Place the zipper in opening, aligning each side. Allow extra length to extend beyond neck.

4 Pin in place. Be generous with the pins, and take all the time you need. Extra care taken here makes the next steps easier.

5 Baste in place. When you are satisfied with the placement, remove the pins.

6 Sew in the zipper, making neat, even stitches that are firm enough to withstand use.

7 Sew a stop at end of zipper and clip excess off if necessary.

8 If the zipper extends beyond the opening, trim extra length.

Measure

Pin

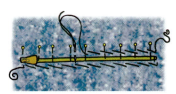

Baste

Sew In

FELTING

To protect your washer from excess fiber, place project in a zippered pillow protector or fine mesh bag. Set washer for hot wash, low water level and maximum agitation. (Using the rinse and spin cycles is not recommended as they may set permanent creases.) Add a small amount of mild detergent, and two old towels (non-shedding) or pairs of jeans for abrasion. Check on the progress about every 5 minutes. Every time you check the progress, pull the project into shape. Reset the washer to continue agitating if necessary. Do not let it drain and spin. When you are happy with the size, remove project from the washer. Rinse thoroughly by hand in cool to warm water. Roll in towels to remove as much water as possible. (Or, for small projects, consider felting by hand. Just dip the knitting in hot, soapy water and then in cold water, rubbing vigorously between each dip. Repeat as many times as necessary until fabric felts.)

Allow to dry completely. Once dry, it may need some grooming to remove any extra fuzz or clumps of wool.

PICK UP AND KNIT VERTICALLY

Insert needle in space *between* first and 2nd stitches.

HORIZONTALLY

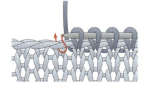

Along a horizontal edge, insert needle into center of every stitch.

PICK-UP RATES

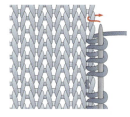

TIP
The ratio of picked-up stitches to rows is based on the pattern's row gauge. It is wise to test the formula by picking up stitches on your gauge swatch, working the border, and binding off.

Example shows picking up 3 stitches for every 4 rows of stockinette stitch.

RIPPING BACK: K1B STITCH

1 Insert left needle into stitch below first stitch on right needle.

2 Remove right needle from stitch, pulling working yarn free. Stitch and float remain.

3 Work the stitch together with the float.

PICKING UP DROPPED K1B STITCHES

1 Insert crochet hook into stitch below dropped stitch.

2 Catch the float as well as the stitch above, and draw the new stitch under the float and through the stitch.

3 Check the reverse side of your work to make sure that your float is secured behind the reconstructed stitch.

Repeat steps 1–3 until only 1 float remains.

Catch last float and pull through stitch.

Slip last stitch onto needle.

Specifications: At a Glance

Use the charts and guides below to make educated decisions about yarn thickness, needle size, garment ease, and pattern options.

Understanding pattern specifications

INTERMEDIATE

C
B | A
STANDARD FIT

S (M, L, 1X, 2X)

A 32 (34½, 40, 45, 48)"
B 26 (27¼, 29, 29, 29¾)"
C 24 (26, 27, 28, 29)"

10cm/4"
22 18
• over Chart for Shell, using larger needles

1 2 3 **4** 5 6
• **Medium weight**
• **500 (600, 700, 800, 900) yds**

• **4.5mm/US 7,**
or size to obtain gauge

&

• **St marker**

◄ *Skill level*

◄ *Fit*
   Includes ease (additional width) built into pattern.

◄ *Sizing*

◄ *Garment measurements*
   at the A, B, and C lines on the fit icon

◄ *Gauge*
   The number of stitches and rows you need in 10 cm or 4", worked as specified.

◄ *Yarn weight*
   and amount in yards

◄ *Type of needles*
   Straight, unless circular or double-pointed are recommended.

◄ *Any extras*

Sizing

Measure around the fullest part of your bust/chest to find your size.

Children	2	4	6	8	10	12	14
Actual chest	21"	23"	25"	26½"	28"	30"	31½"

Women	XXS	XS	Small	Medium	Large	1X	2X	3X
Actual bust	28"	30"	32–34"	36–38"	40–42"	44–46"	48–50"	52–54"

Men	Small	Medium	Large	1X	2X
Actual chest	34–36"	38–40"	42–44"	46–48"	50–52"

Fit

B | A
VERY CLOSE FIT
actual bust/ chest size

C
B | A
CLOSE FIT
actual bust/chest size plus 1–2"

C
B | A
STANDARD FIT
bust/chest plus 2–4"

C
B | A
LOOSE FIT
bust/chest plus 4–6"

C
B | A
OVERSIZED FIT
bust/chest plus 6" or more

Measuring

• **A** Bust/Chest
• **B** Body length
• **C** Center back to cuff (arm slightly bent)

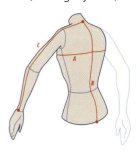

Needles/Hooks

US	MM	HOOK
0	2	A
1	2.25	B
2	2.75	C
3	3.25	D
4	3.5	E
5	3.75	F
6	4	G
7	4.5	7
8	5	H
9	5.5	I
10	6	J
10½	6.5	K
11	8	L
13	9	M
15	10	N
17	12.75	

Equivalent weights

¾	oz	20 g
1	oz	28 g
1½	oz	40 g
1¾	oz	50 g
2	oz	60 g
3½	oz	100 g

Conversion chart

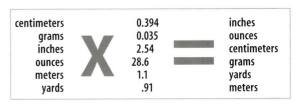

centimeters	0.394		inches
grams	0.035		ounces
inches	2.54		centimeters
ounces	28.6		grams
meters	1.1		yards
yards	.91		meters

Project Yarns

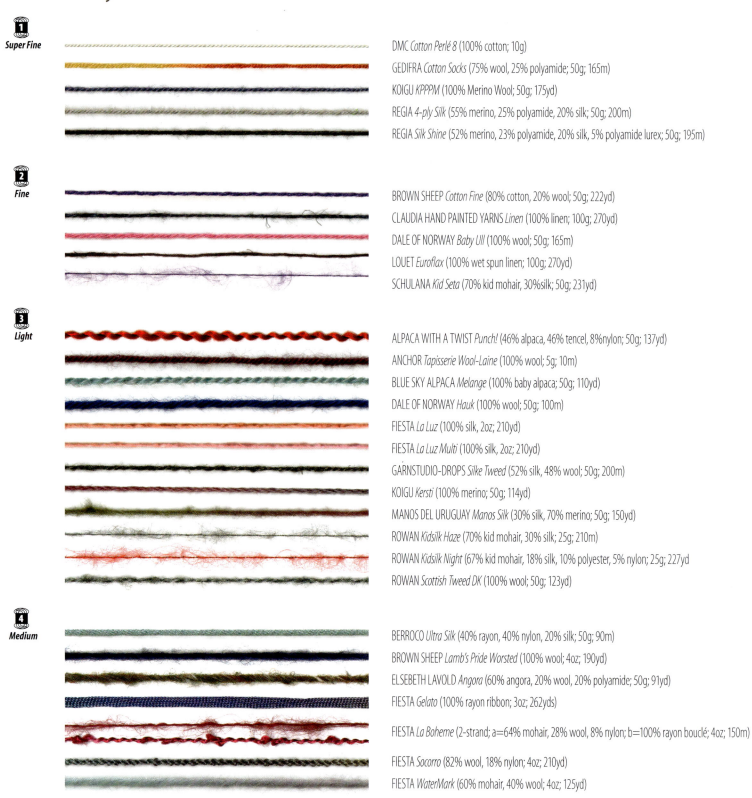

1 Super Fine

DMC *Cotton Perlé 8* (100% cotton; 10g)

GEDIFRA *Cotton Socks* (75% wool, 25% polyamide; 50g; 165m)

KOIGU *KPPPM* (100% Merino Wool; 50g; 175yd)

REGIA *4-ply Silk* (55% merino, 25% polyamide, 20% silk; 50g; 200m)

REGIA *Silk Shine* (52% merino, 23% polyamide, 20% silk, 5% polyamide lurex; 50g; 195m)

2 Fine

BROWN SHEEP *Cotton Fine* (80% cotton, 20% wool; 50g; 222yd)

CLAUDIA HAND PAINTED YARNS *Linen* (100% linen; 100g; 270yd)

DALE OF NORWAY *Baby Ull* (100% wool; 50g; 165m)

LOUET *Euroflax* (100% wet spun linen; 100g; 270yd)

SCHULANA *Kid Seta* (70% kid mohair, 30%silk; 50g; 231yd)

3 Light

ALPACA WITH A TWIST *Punch!* (46% alpaca, 46% tencel, 8%nylon; 50g; 137yd)

ANCHOR *Tapisserie Wool-Laine* (100% wool; 5g; 10m)

BLUE SKY ALPACA *Melange* (100% baby alpaca; 50g; 110yd)

DALE OF NORWAY *Hauk* (100% wool; 50g; 100m)

FIESTA *La Luz* (100% silk, 2oz; 210yd)

FIESTA *La Luz Multi* (100% silk, 2oz; 210yd)

GARNSTUDIO-DROPS *Silke Tweed* (52% silk, 48% wool; 50g; 200m)

KOIGU *Kersti* (100% merino; 50g; 114yd)

MANOS DEL URUGUAY *Manos Silk* (30% silk, 70% merino; 50g; 150yd)

ROWAN *Kidsilk Haze* (70% kid mohair, 30% silk; 25g; 210m)

ROWAN *Kidsilk Night* (67% kid mohair, 18% silk, 10% polyester, 5% nylon; 25g; 227yd)

ROWAN *Scottish Tweed DK* (100% wool; 50g; 123yd)

4 Medium

BERROCO *Ultra Silk* (40% rayon, 40% nylon, 20% silk; 50g; 90m)

BROWN SHEEP *Lamb's Pride Worsted* (100% wool; 4oz; 190yd)

ELSEBETH LAVOLD *Angora* (60% angora, 20% wool, 20% polyamide; 50g; 91yd)

FIESTA *Gelato* (100% rayon ribbon; 3oz; 262yds)

FIESTA *La Boheme* (2-strand; a=64% mohair, 28% wool, 8% nylon; b=100% rayon bouclé; 4oz; 150m)

FIESTA *Socorro* (82% wool, 18% nylon; 4oz; 210yd)

FIESTA *WaterMark* (60% mohair, 40% wool; 4oz; 125yd)

Yarn weight categories

Yarn Weight

1	2	3	4	5	6
Super Fine	**Fine**	**Light**	**Medium**	**Bulky**	**Super Bulky**

Also called

Sock Fingering Baby	Sport Baby	DK Light- Worsted	Worsted Afghan Aran	Chunky Craft Rug	Bulky Roving

Locate the Yarn Weight and Stockinette Stitch Gauge Range over 10cm to 4" on the chart. Compare that range with the information on the yarn label to find an appropriate yarn. These are guidelines only for commonly used gauges and needle sizes in specific yarn categories.

Stockinette Stitch Gauge Range 10cm/4 inches

27 sts to 32 sts	23 sts to 26 sts	21 sts to 24 sts	16 sts to 20 sts	12 sts to 15 sts	6 sts to 11 sts

Recommended needle (metric)

2.25 mm to 3.25 mm	3.25 mm to 3.75 mm	3.75 mm to 4.5 mm	4.5 mm to 5.5 mm	5.5 mm to 8 mm	8 mm and larger

Recommended needle (US)

1 to 3	3 to 5	5 to 7	7 to 9	9 to 11	11 and larger

FLEECE ARTIST *Woolie Silk 3-ply* (65% wool, 35% wilk; 100g; 230m))

GREAT ADIRONDACK *Crêpe* (79% wool, 18% nylon, 3% metal; 114g; 200yd)

LANG YARNS *Pearl* (42% kid mohair, 54% acrylic, 4% polyester; 50g; 105m)

MISSION FALLS *1824 Cotton* (100% cotton; 50g; 85yd)

MISSION FALLS *1824 Wool* (100% merino superwash; 50g; 85yd)

MANOS DEL URUGUAY *Manos Wool Classica* (100% pure wool; 100g; 183yd)

MOUNTAIN COLORS *Alpaca Blend* (50% superfine alpaca, 50% wool; 7oz; 440yd)

NASHUA HANDKNITS *Creative Focus Worsted* (75% wool, 25% alpaca, 100g; 220yd)

NASHUA HANDKNITS *Wooly Stripes* (100% wool; 50g; 88yd)

NORO *Kochoran* (50% wool, 30% angora, 20% silk, 100g; 176yd)

NORO *Kureyon* (100% wool; 50g; 110yd)

NORO *Silk Garden* (45% silk, 45% mohair, 10% wool; 50g; 122yd)

PRISM *Tencel Tape* (100% tencel; 2oz; 120yd)

TAHKI•STACY CHARLES *127 print* (100% wool; 50g; 85m)

TAHKI•STACY CHARLES *Zara Plus* (100% Merino; 50g; 77yd)

5
Bulky

GREAT ADIRONDACK *Apollo* (50% silk, 50% wool; 114g; 160yd)

LANG YARNS *Tosca* (55% wool, 45% acrylic; 50g; 92m)

NASHUA HANDKNITS *Vignette* (100% superwash wool; 50g; 93yd)

REYNOLD'S *Lopi* (100% Icelandic wool, 100g; 110yd)

ZITRON *Loft* (100% merino; 50g; 100m)

I am greatly indebted to a number of people who, in one form or another, made a valuable contribution to this book and without whom this book might never have been written. They helped by providing inspiration and suggestions, by knitting garments and critiquing the text. In alphabetical order by first name, they are: Ada Jackson, Dana Gibbons, Diane Martin, Elizabeth Hulse, Gloria Williams, Janet Kallstrom, Joan Kass, John Allen, Karen Frisa, Monique Fourcaudot, Sandra Whittaker, Svetlana Avrakh and, last but not least, Wannietta Prescod, Canada's fastest knitter, without whom deadlines would have become dead ends.

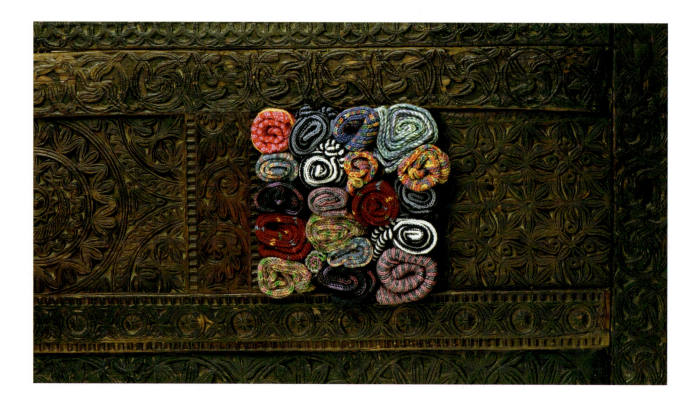

My heartfelt thanks also go out to Elaine Rowley, my indefatigable editor, whose attention to detail was the keystone to holding it all together, and to Alexis Xenakis who, with his artistry in photography, breathed life into my projects. I would also like express my gratitude to the highly professional people at XRX, Beth Whiteside, Bob Natz, Carol Skallerud, Dennis Pearson, Elisabeth Robinson, Everett Baker, Greg Hoogeveen, Karen Bright, Lisa Mannes, Rick Mondragon and Sue Nelson, all of whom assisted in their areas of expertise through every step of the entire project.

And wrapping up this list, to L.D., who wishes to remain anonymous.